2.23.71

# GETTING IT TOGETHER

# GETTING IT TOGETHER

A Guide to Modern
Psychological Analysis

## ROBERT B. EWEN

Franklin Watts    New York    London    1976

**Library of Congress Cataloging in Publication Data**

Ewen, Robert B     1940–
  Getting it together.

  Bibliography: p.
  Includes index.
  SUMMARY: An introduction to the techniques of psychological analysis: how to recognize one's hang-ups, what causes them, and how to seek professional help.
  1. Neuroses—Juvenile literature. 2. Psychotherapy—Juvenile literature. [1. Neuroses. 2. Psychotherapy] I. Title. [DNLM: 1. Neuroses—Etiology—Popular works. 2. Neuroses—Therapy—Popular works. 3. Psychology, Applied—Popular works. WM170 E94g]
RC530.E88    616.8′9    75-25580
ISBN 0-531-01109-7

"Why do I have to serve such a long sentence for the crime of being a coward [Roberta asked]? All I really ever did wrong in my life was to be afraid of being myself." . . . It suddenly struck me how so many of my patients, like Roberta, spent their lives reacting to a feeling from a forgotten event, a feeling whose source was obscure but would be felt whether they wanted to feel it or not. And unless they found out where the disconnected feeling came from and measured it, it would make them distort the world around and inside themselves and they would begin to lose their sense of what was real.

—David S. Viscott,
*The Making of a Psychiatrist*

# Contents

# Preface

This book explains how some of the most common kinds of neurotic hang-ups are caused, how they direct a person's behavior without the person's even being aware of them, and how they can be reduced or eliminated. Although the case material is entirely new, there is nothing radical about the theory; in fact, some of these ideas were developed many years ago. Unfortunately, psychology is not getting through to the general public nearly as well as it should.

These are troubled times, and a strong effort must be made to resolve the personal hang-ups from which societal and international hang-ups develop. I strongly believe that our best chance lies in making techniques of psychological analysis more widely understood. Thus the purpose of this book is to provide fundamental information about perhaps the most fascinating of all topics—our own minds and personalities.

Robert B. Ewen

# GETTING IT TOGETHER

# 1

# Neurosis and Selective Stupidity

Though obviously intelligent in some ways, [the person with neurotic hang-ups] is stupid insofar as his neurotic conflict is concerned. This stupidity is not an overall affair, however. It is really a stupid area in the mind of a person who is quite intelligent in other respects.

—John Dollard and Neal E. Miller,
*Personality and Psychotherapy*

What does a full-fledged neurosis feel like? Let's listen to Roy,* who has suffered from this form of psychopathology for most of his thirty years:

*I walk down the street always in a cold sweat, hoping no one will see me. I'm afraid all the time; my stomach churns and my vision is so obscured by my emotions that I don't recognize even familiar and friendly faces that happen to come into view. It feels crazy to be in*

*A pseudonym, as are all names used in case studies in this book.

*such pain without any apparent reason; after all, there are people who are starving, or crippled, or treated like dirt by bigots, or even killed. So, guilty and confused, I hide my true feelings and structure my mental world narrowly around myself like a cocoon, keeping my thoughts, emotions, and perceptions within a narrow shell because I don't see any hope for me in the outside world and I just want to avoid hurting any more than I do now.*

*I shy away from other people and spend lots of time alone in my room. When other people do invite me out, it usually works out very badly; I have so little sense of who I am and what I want that I'm terribly vulnerable to their wishes and often find myself doing things I can't stand, which makes me even more determined to be alone in the future. I do have a respected, well-paid job that I like to think of as one of my strengths, but at work I can't seem to stop doing things to tear myself down. At conferences I'm likely to make a silly remark that makes me feel ridiculous; with colleagues I feel painfully and terribly inferior; and with subordinates I often become unreasonably angry and irritated. And while I'm usually afraid to admit this to myself because it seems so weird, my work seems like a game I'm playing and observing with a small fraction of my mind, while most of my attention is tied up by the emotional turmoil going on inside me. In fact, I usually feel like an empty shell going through the motions of talking, listening, or behaving; I suspect that something is desperately wrong with me, but that something seems so strange and frightening that I don't dare look for it.*

*Things are bad enough without other people thinking that I'm crazy, so I hide how lost and confused I feel from everyone else. This has become so much of a habit that I'm hardly aware I'm hiding anything; I think of myself as open and honest, and I can't understand why others don't know where my head is at and don't treat me the way I'd like. I guess you could say that I've surrounded myself with self-deception so that I'll have at least some feeling of standing tall, even though it feels more like standing on a ground of quicksand. Yet, deep inside me, I can't help wondering: What went wrong? How did I get to be like this? Isn't there anything that can be done to help me?*

Roy's story illustrates that the victim of neurosis lives in a never-ending nightmare—a personal hell just as painful as the horrors of drug addiction or alcoholism, and one that is even more troublesome to other individuals and to society. Neurosis afflicts some ten million Americans, making it the single most common form of mental disorder. In fact, all of us are at least somewhat neurotic—perhaps not so seriously as Roy, but enough to have hang-ups that cause pain for ourselves, those we love, friends, co-workers, and (in the case of political leaders) even entire nations.

## The Problem of Faulty Learning: 2 + 2 = 5

Roy's case is important because he, like most people, is a victim of *selective stupidity.* Despite the fact that his IQ is around the genius level, Roy behaves like a mental defective when faced with certain important situations. The reason for this, and for much of Roy's emotional pain, is that he has been led astray by *faulty learning* about the nature of his own true self and the world around him.

If society taught children how to know and understand themselves with the same zeal that it teaches them spelling and arithmetic, the incidence of neurosis would be greatly reduced. Let's suppose that either because of poor teaching or your misunderstanding, you learn that $2 + 2 = 5$. This causes you to keep getting wrong answers on your homework, punishment from your teacher, and derision from your classmates, and your self-esteem therefore lurches toward zero. And if none of the people to whom you show your homework is able to figure out the true nature of your "delusion," you will go through life victimized by faulty learning and beset by failure.

Schools do, of course, correct such foolish and potentially harmful notions as $2 + 2 = 5$. However, nothing is done to help a child recognize and change equally faulty ideas about a far more important topic—himself or herself. Roy, who can solve mathematical equations that would give most people severe headaches, has been misled throughout life by mistaken ideas about himself and his world that he learned as a child and never corrected, such as:

I am unlovable and basically worthless.
I have no right to do what I really want.
I must never quit anything; quitting is shameful.
The best way to avoid pain is to stay by myself and
    avoid other people.

Once, after following his fourth rule for several months and finding himself lonely and upset, he decided to risk going to a party. Unfortunately, it turned out to be unpleasant and anxiety-provoking. A person not victimized by neurotic hang-ups would resolve that problem simply by leaving the party, but not Roy; his misguided rules of life interfered. "I have no right to do what I really want," he thought. "How can I leave so early? My host might be offended. Everyone would think I was no good because I quit. My parents would feel that I wasn't giving other people a fair chance. My analyst would say that I didn't make enough of an attempt to improve my social life." The result was that Roy behaved very ineptly: he wandered back and forth between the door and the party, unable to decide whether to stay or leave; he was nervous, boring, and irritating in his few contacts with other people, partly because of his painful conflict and partly in an unconscious attempt to get them to resolve his dilemma by kicking him out; and he finally stayed grimly until the end, vowing never to go to any more parties in the future. Roy's helplessness in this actually simple situation is an excellent example of selective stupidity.

Faulty rules of the kind that victimize Roy begin in early childhood. Sometimes they develop even before the child's use of language is mastered. Roy has been living by his misguided rules for so long that he no longer understands them very well and cannot identify them accurately; in fact, he has never in his life put some of them into words. Obviously, this makes it extremely difficult for him to change them. And to make matters worse, he is likely to regard these rules as life-*saving* and cling to them desperately, not realizing that they are the source of his intense emotional pain. Thus, his decision not to attend any more parties seems to him like an essential (and clever) method of self-protection; but the result will be considerable loneliness and additional misery.

Roy's case is extreme, but the kind of reasoning that is involved does pertain to the neurotic hang-ups that we all have. As with Roy, our hang-ups hurt us and those close to us; we have more than enough intelligence to solve our emotional problems, but we are pushed around by faulty rules of life that make us selectively stupid; and we tend to regard these rules as essential to our survival and refuse to give them up without a struggle, even though they are actually hurting us.

The goal of this book is to explain how to identify, understand, and resolve neurotic hang-ups. It should be noted, however, that changing oneself is a difficult and challenging undertaking. To be sure, more than a few authors and publishers attempt to cash in on people's emotional suffering by producing sugar-coated prescriptions for instant rapture, something like "How to Stop Being Neurotic and Become Deliriously Happy in Six Easy Lessons." It would indeed be nice if a set of glib and entertaining rules sufficed to overcome problems and change behavior patterns of many years' standing, but common sense should indicate that this isn't very likely. Instead, this book will deal with the one approach that is most likely to be successful—one based on established principles of modern clinical psychology.

# 2
# The Origins of Neurotic Hang-ups

When a child is forced to prove himself as capable [to his parents], results are often disastrous. A child needs love, acceptance and understanding. He is devastated when confronted with rejection, doubts, and never-ending testing.

—Virginia M. Axline,
*Dibs in Search of Self*

. . . there is great temptation to overprotect [the only child]. When he calls, the parents run; when he whimpers, they are abashed; when he is sick, they are guilty; when he doesn't sleep, they look as though *they* are going to have nervous breakdowns. . . . all this attention actually amounts to a considerable *curtailing* of the child's freedom, and he must, like a prince born into a royal family, carry a weight for which children were never made.

—Rollo May,
*Love and Will*

Neurotic hang-ups have their origins in a person's early life—infancy, childhood, and (to a lesser extent) adolescence. There are two major reasons why the young child is very vulnerable to the faulty learning that sows the seeds of neurosis:

1. The child's misperceptions. A young child is naïve and inexperienced in the art of living, unable to use language well, and motivated by some irrational and unrealis-

tic wishes (such as the need for perfect and all-powerful parents). Therefore the child is likely to distort or misperceive what is actually happening and be unable to recall the results of these learning experiences at a later date.

2. The child's dependence on the parents. A young child is helpless, and therefore dependent on his or her parents; and the parents, because of their own neurotic hang-ups, actually (if inadvertently) teach the child to be neurotic.

### The Child's Misperceptions

Very young children are likely to misunderstand what is going on around them because they know so little about life. And since they have not yet learned to use language well, they cannot *label* the events that occur—or the emotions and beliefs that result—by using the appropriate words. This prevents them from correcting faulty learning by talking to their parents; and it also makes it very hard for them to remember erroneous ideas so that they can correct them when they are older. Thus many early experiences and their effects become *unconscious,* and direct one's behavior from then on without one even realizing it.*

For example, if a loved one disappears, an adult can readily distinguish among such possible causes as death, deliberate desertion, and unwilling and temporary departure. And an adult can usually identify the emotions that would result from this event, such as helplessness, sorrow, and anger. This is due partly to experience in living and partly to the ability to assign a different label (name) to each concept. A young child cannot do this, however, and the faulty learning that can result may lead to serious hang-ups.

*Memories, emotions, beliefs, and motives that originate when a person *is* old enough to use language well can also become unconscious. This occurs through the use of defense mechanisms, which are discussed in the next chapter.

Roy, whose neurosis involved typical feelings of self-hate and worthlessness, was able to use his adult abilities to track down one of the childhood causes of his low self-esteem:

*I've always known that one of the most traumatic incidents in my life was when my father was drafted; I was only three at the time, and we had been very close. My parents tried to explain what was happening, but the concept of the draft was incomprehensible to me. So, when my father said good-bye to me at the door, I only sensed dimly that this was very different from similar occasions. Maybe because I wanted to believe it, I decided that he was just going shopping at a nearby store and would be back soon. But it was nine months—a period that seemed like an eternity—before I saw him again. Now, as an adult, I understand about the draft, and I know that he didn't leave willingly or because he didn't love me; but though I've explained that to myself for years, it never seemed to help very much.*

*At this point, my thinking really got bogged down. I had been taken in by a red herring; I was concentrating so hard on the concept of the draft that I ignored factors that were actually far more important—my own behavior at the time, and the emotions and beliefs that resulted. It wasn't until an important incident occurred in my current life that I was finally able to work out the solution, and this happened as follows: I had just mailed an angry and impulsive letter to a colleague, one I soon regretted sending. Talking the matter over with a third party, I pointed out that I should have waited a few days and cooled off before deciding whether or not to send the letter, but I "just knew" that I couldn't afford even a five-minute delay. My friend then suggested that at some time in my life I had wanted to tell someone something very important but had missed my chance because I waited too long, with the result that I was now being pushed around by unconscious memories of that experience.*

*This was the clue I'd been searching for, and applying it to the draft incident was really enlightening. I now realized that when my father said good-bye at the door, I wanted to run to him for a good-bye hug and tell him that I loved him very much and was sorry that he was going, but I didn't. Even now, I can feel how much I wanted that hug! My failure to realize that he would be gone for a long time, and that this was therefore my last chance, made me feel stupid; and not showing my emotions made me feel like a coward. But words and concepts like "stupid" and "coward" were beyond me at that age, so I felt only a strong and long-lasting self-hate that I never understood until now. (In fact, when I finally did see my father again, I unconsciously reversed my complaint and blamed him for not saying good-bye to me!) I also "learned" that there's no way to make up for an error; my father was gone for so long that I couldn't recoup by giving him that hug a little later. That's one reason why I'm always so afraid of making mistakes, and explode in anger or sulk when I do make them.*

Roy's feelings of self-hate stemmed from more than just this one incident, painful as it was; strong beliefs or habitual behaviors are likely to have multiple causes. Even so, his unraveling of this one issue did help to increase his self-esteem. Agreeing that his inexperience as a child offered extenuating circumstances for his behavior, he was able to take a more compassionate and sympathetic view toward himself. One result was that his relationship with his father improved, further easing his feelings of guilt. Finally, Roy now takes his inevitable errors much more in stride because he is no longer victimized by the unconscious belief that they can never be corrected—or, to put it another way, he is no longer selectively stupid in this particular area.

Here's another example:

*Carol's father died after a long illness when she was very young. She had to walk softly all the time so as not to disturb the invalid, while never getting the love, warmth, and physical affection that she craved. The concept of terminal illness was incomprehensible to her at that age, so she couldn't understand why he denied her his love; and the emotions and beliefs that resulted were never labeled properly because she was too young to know the right words. Her inexperience with life and language made it impossible for Carol to identify and remember what she had "learned": that men will never be around when she needs them; that men don't have any love and warmth to offer and, in fact, are actually nuisances that have to be catered to; that she must be a pretty worthless person to be denied love from her own father; and that by doing (or not doing) some-*

*thing, she herself was responsible for losing the love that she wanted so much.*

Unfortunately, Carol's case does not have a happy ending, for she never learned how to detect and change her own hang-ups. To this day, she rarely dates; and when she does go out, her irrational bursts of anger, evident nervousness, and excessive demands on the man to prove his loyalty soon drive away anyone who might be interested in her. Thus Carol, who is an intelligent woman, remains selectively stupid in her dealings with men—an extremely painful hang-up due in large part to the faulty learning that took place during her relationship with her invalid father.

Major incidents in one's early childhood that often lead to a substantial amount of faulty learning include the loss of a parent through death, divorce, or desertion; the birth or death of a sibling; early feeding habits; how toilet training is handled; how the parents react to the child's natural exploration of his or her sexual organs; how the parents react to the child's displays of anger, aggression, and independence; and any other event that arouses strong feelings. Memory is often fallible, so it's desirable to check up on childhood events by talking with those who were present during their occurrence. Also, it's important to analyze the *emotions, beliefs, and motives* that result from these experiences. Thinking about the unfairness of the draft, or about his father's reasons for leaving, didn't help Roy very much; he began to feel better only after he figured out that it was his own behavior, and his own emotions and beliefs, that caused his painful feelings of self-hate. Finally, these examples also indicate the value of relating present disturbances to childhood events. Roy's haste to send an angry letter, which he himself recognized as excessive, provided the key that helped unlock a twenty-five-year-old mystery. Carol, had she been able to relate her unreasonable anger with men she dated to her traumatic experiences with her father, might well have begun to understand herself—and find some enjoyment in her relationships with males.

## Parental Neurotic Behaviors

All children begin life as helpless infants who are totally dependent upon other people. There are times when infants cry from hunger but are not fed, or want attention but are ignored, or soil themselves but are not changed, thus emphasizing to them that they are unable to satisfy their own needs.

Since we do not yet have a perfect science of child-rearing, all of us become at least a little neurotic. That is, we all have at least some unconscious feelings of self-contempt which we have never labeled and which therefore continue to influence our behavior without our being aware of it. If sufficient warmth, love, and reassurance are provided during childhood, there is every chance that a person will grow up with relatively few neurotic hang-ups. When the child's parents are themselves neurotic, however, real trouble will occur. As a result of their own faulty learning during childhood, such parents are extremely insecure and anxious about their own worth. They are thus threatened by any behavior of the child that they regard as challenging their own adequacy. For them, being a parent is only a task to succeed at, rather than an opportunity to be enjoyed. Unfortunately, those who are most afraid of making mistakes are most likely to make them; and parents who are driven by the goal of avoiding failure ultimately teach the child to feel frightened and unreal and to have severe doubts as to his or her worth as a human being.

### OVERPROTECTIVENESS AND REJECTION

Two common forms of parental neurotic behavior, overprotectiveness and rejection, frequently occur together.

The likely result is an adult who has great difficulty showing initiative, making decisions, and experimenting with
different aspects of life in order to find his or her own thing.
Roy's case serves as a good illustration:

> When I was very young, my parents told me never to walk through
> the kitchen. This seemed pretty silly to me; the quickest way to get
> from the dining room to my room was through the kitchen, and I saw
> every day that nothing bad ever happened there. So one day I broke
> the rule while they were watching, to show them what I thought. I
> was proud of myself for a minute, but then my parents said how
> disappointed they were in me and turned their backs on me in dis-
> gust. I was shattered; I felt all alone, like I'd been kicked out of my
> own family. Recently, when I asked my parents about this, they
> explained that they had read a newspaper story about a kitchen
> stove blowing up in an apartment down the street. "What else could
> we do?" they argued. "It was our responsibility as parents to protect
> you."
>
> Thinking back over my life, I found many other instances when
> my parents were overprotective. In fact, they were always nervous
> about the possibility of something happening to me. So I learned
> never to show any initiative, because I "knew" I'd get wiped out if I
> did. I learned that the only thing in life that really mattered, and that
> would keep my parents' love, was to be safe; I had no right to take
> any chances at all, even if I felt miserable. And avoiding risks
> wasn't easy, what with the world being a terrifying place with unex-
> plained danger even in my own kitchen. But I was too young to put
> these rules of life into words, so they became unconscious—and
> have been directing my behavior ever since.

There are several important points to be gleaned from
this example:

1. *Overprotectiveness destroys a child's initiative and
self-esteem.* Testing reality, which includes making mistakes and learning from them, enables a child to find out
about the world. Because of their anxieties, Roy's parents
denied him this opportunity; and their overprotectiveness
taught him to fear the unknown and distrust his ability to
deal with it.

2. *Rejection is a severe and misguided form of punishment.* Since the inexperienced child has difficulty distin-

guishing between temporary rejection and permanent desertion, rejection can be much more terrifying than a slap or spanking. Rather than teaching the child not to break the rules, it may totally squelch all forms of initiative and independence. In fact, psychological punishments such as rejection, sarcasm, or ridicule can hurt far more than spankings.

3. *Parental hypocrisy, whether conscious or unconscious, makes a child feel confused and threatened.* The hang-ups that victimized Roy's parents were unconscious, so they saw their own behavior as normal loving concern—and described it that way to Roy. As a result, he concluded that his natural desires to show initiative and take chances were wrong and abnormal. He also learned to equate love from people with the pain of having his own wishes and individuality taken from him, another powerful unlabeled belief that seriously affected his interpersonal relationships.

4. *Crucial childhood incidents reflect lifelong patterns of parent-child interaction.* Once he came to appreciate the significance of the kitchen incident, Roy was able to identify many other instances where his parents' overprotectiveness taught him to feel afraid and incompetent. Neurotic hang-ups do *not* normally result from one specific childhood event; such important experiences are significant because they are major indications of how the parents behaved throughout the child's formative years.

5. *The child's own errors make a bad situation worse.* Roy found it easy to overlook the fact that his breaking a rule did call for punishment, and that his misperceiving the true nature of that punishment made it seem much more painful. Some people find it tempting to blame their hang-ups entirely on their parents, but this is self-defeating. As Roy himself now puts it: "It's hard to give up being the innocent victim overcome with righteous anger, but it's actually worth it. As long as I see myself as a helpless child

totally controlled by other people's errors, I can't begin to take steps to improve my own life. Acknowledging that I made a mistake may hurt, but it's a lot better than feeling like there's no 'I' at all!''

## CONSTANT ANXIETY

Extreme anxiety is often learned from parents who were themselves constantly nervous. Such parents are driven by unconscious but highly threatening feelings of inadequacy and self-contempt that they learned during their own childhood. Therefore they are overly sensitive to any behavior of the child that may reflect badly on them. If the child should get hurt, his pain becomes an occasion for self-reproach or even panic rather than love and sympathy. Or relatively minor misbehavior or failure by the child causes the parents to feel so threatened that they read the riot act instead of providing the reassurance and relaxed atmosphere that the child desperately needs. Thus the child is taught the parents' insecurities; the world becomes a dangerous and frightening place where a single slip can mean disaster; and neurotic anxiety has been handed down once again from one generation to the next. Roy's experiences are typical:

> My mother always reacted to any pain and unhappiness of mine with nervous irritation, rather than with warmth and comfort. When I broke a favorite toy and cried, she got annoyed and told me to forget about it. She promised to replace the toy, but never did; she was just trying to get rid of the incident (and my feelings) as quickly as possible. The same thing happened when she once dropped a heavy can of juice on my foot. It really hurt; but instead of being sympathetic, she got upset and told me to ignore it. So I learned that when I get hurt, or when I break something of mine, my pain and regrets don't matter to anybody; in fact, they're a source of annoyance to my parents. Without consciously realizing it, I decided that I'd better go to any lengths to avoid injuring myself or damaging anything of my own that I cared about.

*My father was very perfectionistic. Once I gave him a paper I'd written for school, expecting a few comments; but he returned it so covered with corrections in glaring red pencil that I felt crushed and stupid. Another time he bawled me out so intensely for being intellectually stupid that I was sick for three days. And all this in spite of the fact that I was an honor student! He was also harsh with anybody who stepped out of line. Once a friend of his (whose son I was friendly with) was found guilty of embezzlement. There was room for compassion, for the way that the man planned the crime was so sick and self-destructive that he had to get caught eventually. But my father, with frightening intensity, let it be known that he'd never again speak to such a despicable person, and I never saw that family again. Because of experiences like these, I've gone through life constantly afraid of making mistakes; but I never understood until now that I was really anxious about making the one misstep that would cost me my father's love.*

The anxiety that results from this kind of faulty learning may have several explanations:

*1. Anxiety may indicate the existence of an unconscious conflict.* Neurotic hang-ups create emotional inner fights, with the result that the person is like a house divided. For example, the person may be in doubt as to his or her own lovability and worth as a person; or one may be in conflict about whether to do one's own thing or follow the dictates of one's parents; or one may be struggling to decide whether to face or avoid a serious problem or threatening belief. In addition to draining a person's energy and making life miserable, constant anxiety causes a person to be selectively stupid when trying to deal with the problem. If the difficulty is of a specific nature, moving away from the situation can make it possible to look things over more calmly and apply one's intelligence more effectively. Mary, a bright college student, developed high anxiety because of an inner conflict stemming from parental pressures:

*I used to shake with nervousness at the prospect of any examination or term paper. Finally, it got so bad that I took a year off from school. Only then did I realize that a leave was what I'd wanted all along; I had hated school, but my parents had been pushing me to*

*stick it out. After loafing for a while and exploring the job market,*
*college began to look pretty good. I went back, this time because I*
*wanted to, and things are much better. I'm still a little anxious about*
*grades, but I can handle it—and I've got a B average.*

2. **Anxiety may indicate the existence of an "extra burden."** Mary's anxiety was also due to the fact that she carried an extra burden with her into the examination room. Faulty learning and parental pressures had taught her that her worth as a human being depended on getting good grades; she was trying to prove not only that she knew the course material but that she was someone who deserved to be loved and valued. This severe additional pressure expressed itself in the form of intense anxiety.

3. **Anxiety may indicate unconscious feelings of guilt.** One reason why Roy was so nervous about going to parties was because he felt guilty about leaving when he wished. He also felt guilty about turning down invitations, since this would indicate that he wasn't trying hard enough to improve his social life. Therefore he went out even when he knew that his hang-ups were still too strong for him to relate to people effectively, did not enjoy himself, and experienced a great deal of anxiety.

4. **Anxiety may reflect the failure to learn needed competencies.** People who grow up with serious hang-ups do tend to miss out on some important aspects of life. For example, they may spend so much time in the safety of their own home (or their own imagination) that they do not learn some of the skills and competencies that are needed in order to get along in the world. They are therefore more likely to fail in certain important areas of their lives and they have some conscious or unconscious realization of this, so they do have some reason to be anxious. They fail to appreciate, however, that they have the capacity to learn now what they need to know—provided that they don't let their fear or guilt about being ignorant or afraid paralyze them into avoiding their problems.

*5. Anxiety may be communicated physically, during infancy, by a nervous mother.* A tense and anxious mother transmits her feelings even to an infant by her shaky touch and inability to provide warmth and comfort. Physical contact with the mother during infancy is extremely important in determining subsequent development, and an infant or child who experiences constant physical tension from the mother will learn to become highly anxious.

### OVERPERMISSIVENESS

By setting limits to the child's behavior, the parents help the child to define the nature of the world and the people in it. If the parents are too insecure to establish any controls and no behavior is punished, the child is likely to learn to do anything to get what he or she wants regardless of how others may feel. Such faulty learning is sure to cause misguided behavior and considerable emotional pain for many people, in later life.

Actually, total overpermissiveness is not that common; being pushed around by one's child is unlikely to be gratifying even to a neurotic parent. However, overpermissiveness is not unusual in combination with other pathological patterns. For example, parents may unfairly overprotect their children, realize this, and engage in a spell of overpermissiveness so as to feel less guilty. Sooner or later, however, the children will push them too far, whereupon the parents will revert to strong discipline. The result is tragic: the overprotective periods teach the children that they dare not do their own thing to get what they want, while the overpermissive treatment shows them that their desires will be satisfied by their parents if they just wait long enough. And while such children may appear "spoiled," they are actually suffering intensely. They need to understand that going after what they want is much more likely to pay off than is waiting for a handout from someone else—and that

putting forth their own efforts is actually much less dangerous than their parents' misguided teaching made it seem.


## HYPOCRISY AND THE DOUBLE BIND

A parent who frequently expresses double messages
that contradict each other causes the child to have serious
hang-ups. Sometimes one message is verbal while the other
consists of facial or bodily expressions or tones of voice.
Alternatively, both messages may be verbal or physical but
occur at different times. This situation, known as the *double bind,* can lead to severe neurosis or even psychosis.
Roy's story provides some excellent examples:

> My parents always told me that they loved me and that I should
> never doubt their love, but there was never any physical affection in
> my family. Instead of hugging, kissing, and spontaneous warmth,
> all I ever saw was constant anxiety and tension. My parents also
> told me frequently that they'd stand behind me no matter what I did,
> but they rejected me and made me feel terribly unloved for the
> slightest mistake. They urged me in words to go out and experience
> life, yet their anxiety and overprotective behavior showed that
> they'd much rather I stayed inside where nothing could happen to
> me. They seemed very strong when they punished me and invited
> me to tell them if they did anything wrong, yet they went to great
> lengths to deny their mistakes and crumbled if I tried to press the
> issue.
>
> A frank discussion of these contradictions might have cleared
> the air, but I was too young to put my feelings into words. So,
> though I didn't consciously realize it, I wound up distrusting both
> the verbal and the physical messages; I didn't know what to believe,
> so I didn't believe anything. And I extended this distrust to other
> people and other situations. After all, if my own parents weren't
> honest, nobody else could be; and if I couldn't figure out the people
> I lived with every day, my own judgment must be totally unreliable.
> After a while, this suspicion about other people and lack of confi-
> dence in my own judgment became so all-pervasive that I felt com-
> fortable only when I was alone.

Roy's self-confidence increased when he came to understand that his childhood judgment was often correct. He

was right when he sensed that his parents, at least in part, did *not* want him to go out or to criticize and evaluate their behavior. And he eventually discovered that his ability to size up and deal with other people and the world was a great deal better than he thought. As a result, people became more approachable and less dangerous, and being in a group became considerably less anxiety-provoking.

### EXCESSIVE GIVING OR TAKING

An important double-bind situation occurs in the area of parental giving and taking. Parents may frequently give their child presents as a concrete way of expressing love. However, because of their own excessive and unresolved need to avoid failure, they constantly take from the child his or her very self; the child must be what they want and do only what will make them happy. Thus the child is losing the most important thing anyone can have, the freedom to be oneself. But the giving of presents helps to prevent any complaints, for the child can hardly object to losing something so intangible as a self when given so much that is real and visible.

The resulting contradiction between giving and taking damages such children's sense of reality and confidence in their own feelings. They sense that they are being taken from, but because so much apparent giving is going on, they don't realize that their judgment is correct. Ultimately they may learn to avoid interpersonal contacts; they fear that others will also rob them of their own true wishes in an unexplained way, and they unconsciously distrust anything nice that others may do for them because they see it as a gift similar to their parents' presents. Thus they are unable to shop the market of interpersonal relationships with any idea that there is something good to get and with any sense of what they want—or, indeed, with any sense of themselves.

Insecure parents may also give frequently to the child because this is one of the rare ways in which they can feel powerful. Attempts by the child to give to them, however, are discouraged—being on the receiving end is a threatening reminder of weakness. So the child never learns to enjoy the strength of giving to his or her own parents and yet another seed of neurotic self-contempt is sown. John got a revealing look at this hang-up at work in someone else's parent:

> I borrowed a man's car for a personal errand. To thank him, I had the gas tank filled before I returned it. His reaction was: "Why'd you do that? What was the matter? Wasn't there enough gas? I was sure there was enough in there when I gave it to you." This man was simply too insecure to accept a favor, and I could only imagine how painful and frustrating this must have been for his son while he was growing up. I'm not at all surprised that the son turned out to be the kind of man who rarely does anything for other people!

Some parents may desperately want a boy (girl) for neurotic or religious reasons, and then proceed to behave in ways that shatter their child's self-esteem if they are unfortunate enough to be "stuck" with a child of the opposite sex. The result is a child who feels manipulated, unloved, angry, and worthless; one who kills himself or herself trying to win the parents' approval, but never succeeds; and one who turns to neurotic solutions in a misguided attempt to restore some shreds of self-confidence.

If a person never learned how to give to other people because the parents were too insecure to accept things in a warm and satisfying way, what can be done to resolve this hang-up? Going through the motions of giving when one doesn't really want to give will only estrange one still further from one's real self. A better plan, therefore, is to try and correct the faulty learning that occurred during childhood. People naturally wish to enjoy the strength of giving to other important people in their lives. Recognizing that these are one's true feelings and abilities, and that it was primarily the parents' hang-ups that caused these impulses to become stifled, enables a person to become a willing and emotionally sincere giver—one who helps others not out of a feeling of guilt or obligation but because it is fun to do so.

If the parents constantly forced the child into unpleasant molds of their own choosing, the sufferer needs to become aware that he or she really was denied the right to develop his or her own personality and style during childhood. A good indication is provided by the quality of the parents' marriage; the more it lacked in emotional warmth and satisfaction, the more likely it is that the parents manipulated the child to satisfy their own needs. If a person habitually shies away from other people and spends a great deal of time alone, hypocritical manipulation by the parents may have caused him or her to distrust people in general. Understanding what actually happened during childhood makes it possible for such people to increase their self-confidence, and then use their judgment to select intimates with whom they can have a truly satisfying relationship.

### THE "CARROT-AND-STICK" APPROACH

Parents who are constantly anxious and insecure cannot reward their child's achievements warmly and fully. Instead, reports of success in school, social life, or whatever are met with a superficially mild reaction that the child interprets as a lack of approval. As a result, the child concludes that he or she must do even better in order to win parental love, and thus establish true self-esteem. However, any future successes are met with the same inhibited response. Thus the child becomes a perfectionist, is never satisfied with his or her own achievements, and constantly sets standards that are beyond reach. There's a scene in a movie called *The Rack* in which a stern military father finally breaks down and embraces his troubled son while saying through his tears, "Was that all you ever wanted?" A warm hug is just what so many neurotic children needed so badly, but were unable to get from their emotionally inhibited parents. Roy puts in this way:

> *I remember when I told my father that I'd made the honor roll for my first semester in high school. I expected something like a cheery smile and a warm hug, but all I got was an expressionless nod. I had thought that my accomplishment was significant in view of the problems involved in adjusting to a new school and the emotional hangups that I sensed I had, but his reaction made me feel that making the honor roll was trivial for someone as bright as I was. Glumly, I decided that I'd have to do even better in the future to get what I wanted from him. But I never labeled my feelings, so I never realized that what I was trying so hard to do was win his love.*

These unconscious feelings cause people to behave in painful and self-destructive ways, as, for example, by choosing a profession that they think their parents want rather than one they'll enjoy. This sale of the soul leads to strong feelings of worthlessness and self-contempt, which they misguidedly try to resolve by working harder. Unfortunately, this anxiety-ridden attempt to live up to someone else's goals cannot fail to produce inefficient behavior, ultimate failure, and still lower self-esteem.

### NEGLECT

Parents may neglect a child either by usually being absent, or by being physically present but emotionally withdrawn and uncommunicative. The stereotype of the parent who is too busy with business or social clubs to attend to the needs of the child, and who tries to make up for this by giving a great many presents, is a common theme in television programs and movies. And as these stories suggest, the faulty learning and self-contempt that result create severe emotional pain and serious neurotic hang-ups. Yet the neglect caused by parents who are physically present, but unable to recognize and respond to the needs of the child, can be equally painful. And because this neglect is less obvious, it can be considerably more difficult to recognize, understand, and resolve.

HEALTHY PARENTAL BEHAVIORS:
A CAUTIONARY NOTE

Neurotic parents are by no means entirely destructive; they do some positive things that make the child feel somewhat loved and somewhat increase the child's self-esteem. This is why Roy never stopped trying to win the love that he considered to be in doubt, no matter how many rebuffs he received because of his parents' neurotic hang-ups. Their positive behaviors suggested that he actually was a worthwhile person who could obtain their love, while their neurotic behaviors taught him that he was *not* good enough and in danger of losing their love at any moment. These contradictory messages led to the unconscious conflict about whether or not he was indeed lovable, and this inner struggle caused the intense and constant anxiety that is typical of severe neurotic hang-ups. Roy failed to realize that his anxiety was a sign of at least some evidence on the positive side of this all-important issue; if his parents' behavior had been entirely bad and unloving, he would have developed a considerably more serious (if less anxious) form of psychopathology such as psychosis or suicidal depression.

## Other Factors

Anyone who was in constant contact or lived with a child's family, such as a grandmother or grandfather, aunt, uncle, brother, or sister, is a likely source of both accurate and faulty learning. In addition, childhood and adolescent peer relationships are also quite important. Roy's story shows how one's own behavior adds fuel to the growing fire of neurosis:

*I thought that I did a good job reading a poem at a school assembly, but my peers made fun of my performance. Only now do I realize that the neurotic intensity I brought to everything I did caused me to act in a way that actually was highly exaggerated. I also got put down for being the teacher's pet and class angel. Because I was so terrified of the one step out of line that would lose my parents' love, I never was able to learn that occasionally breaking the rules is desirable in order to be accepted by one's classmates. Similarly, my neurotic safety needs made me behave like a coward on those occasions when I did go out with my peers. But I didn't understand my own behavior and the faulty learning that caused it, so I concluded that other people were basically hostile. I also decided that, as I'd suspected all along, I myself was fundamentally unlikable. In despair I gave up the idea of ever having good friends, or ever being loved.*

This example is typical of how hang-ups trigger vicious circles that actively make the sufferer's life worse. The past is far from the only important factor in neurotic hang-ups; its residues cause self-destructive behavior in the here and now.

# 3

# Defense Mechanisms

... a person [with neurotic hang-ups] builds up
an idealized image of himself because he cannot
tolerate himself as he actually is. The image apparently counteracts this calamity; but having
placed himself on a pedestal, he can tolerate his
real self still less and starts to rage against it, to
despise himself and to chafe under the yoke of
his own unattainable demands upon himself. He
wavers then between self-adoration and self-contempt, between his idealized image and his de-
spised image, with no solid middle ground to fall
back on.

—Karen Horney,
*Our Inner Conflicts*

Persons who have been subjected to parental neurotic
behaviors and anxieties, buffeted by contradictory double-
bind messages, taught that normal attempts to develop initiative and a sense of self are betrayals that will cost them
parental love, and victimized by their own naïve misperceptions will come to live in a constant state of anxiety.
Because the world seems so incomprehensible, they are in
perpetual fear that the other shoe will drop at any moment.

And since they have learned to distrust their own capacity to deal with their environment, they feel hopelessly inadequate to improve their painful situation. Eventually, anxiety and self-contempt become so acute that all of their energy is devoted to the search for safety and relief from emotional pain; and this goal is sought at any cost, even to the point of sacrificing their own true wishes and desires. Like prisoners of war or victims of concentration camps, they are preoccupied with surviving from day to day. The pursuit of happiness is for them unthinkable.

In their quest for relief, people with neurotic hang-ups unconsciously adopt one or more *defense mechanisms.* Unconscious defense mechanisms are the heroin on which neurotics become hooked and which, like drugs, temporarily make them feel better but ultimately make matters far worse.

## Repression

Repression consists of unconsciously eliminating unpleasant or threatening beliefs, thoughts, emotions, motives, or memories from one's awareness, with the result that they cannot be brought to consciousness on demand. For example, a person may temporarily reduce anxiety and restore a modicum of self-esteem by repressing his belief that his parents don't really love him (and that he is therefore basically unlovable) and the childhood incidents that caused this feeling.

As with all defense mechanisms, the cure is usually worse than the disease. Since repression conceals the true factors that are directing a person's behavior, the likely result is that the person will choose misguided goals—ones that may seem attractive from a distance, but which turn out to be dissatisfying. Such ill-judged choices are also likely to lead to failure, criticism from others (and from oneself), and increased feelings of self-contempt and dependence on defense mechanisms. The ultimate result is a *vicious circle* wherein matters get still worse because they are getting worse. (See Figure 1.)

Since repressed material cannot be recalled on demand, special techniques are necessary to bring it to light. These include investigation into one's childhood, dream analysis (see Chapter 5), and certain formal psychotherapeutic techniques (see Chapter 7).

### Reaction Formation

Repression often occurs along with other defense mechanisms, one of which is reaction formation. If certain feelings, beliefs, memories, or motives are threatening and anxiety-provoking, one way of obtaining temporary relief is unconsciously to adopt substitutes that are far removed from—in fact, diametrically opposed to—the offending ones. For example, a person who has learned to feel extremely anxious and guilty about any direct expressions of anger and aggression may become an outspoken pacifist. Or one may become a crusader against sexual immorality or alcohol abuse in order to conceal from oneself the anxiety that one has learned to associate with personal desires for sex or liquor. Or a person may slave away at a job, or refuse to delegate tasks to willing subordinates, to conceal the fact that he or she really hates the work and would like to chuck the whole thing and quit. Or a patient may become furious at the car or train that breaks down and causes him or her to miss a psychotherapy session in order to hide the fact that this person really does not want to be in therapy at all, but is too weak to quit against the therapist's wishes. In each case, the newly adopted behaviors or beliefs reduce anxiety and restore some self-esteem because they are as far removed as possible from the true, threatening ones.

Since reaction formation represents so fundamental a denial of a person's true self, it ultimately leads to severe

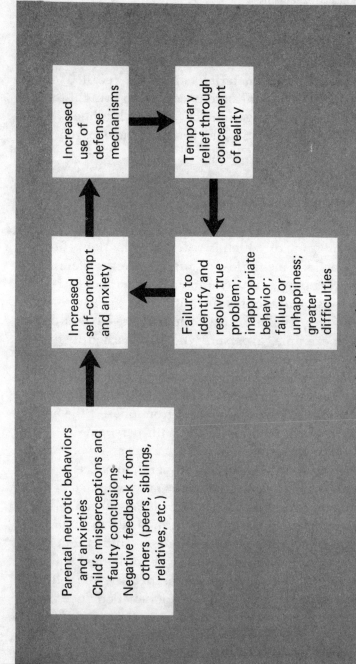

Figure 1.  The fundamental neurotic vicious circle

difficulties. Charles was respected by his friends because he was a doctor and a teacher, but his own inner feelings were an entirely different matter:

> *My childhood and adolescence led me to believe that none of my peers really liked me. Since this was too painful to think about, I unconsciously repressed it. Naturally, I felt angry and disinclined to give a damn about anybody else, but I couldn't face those emotions; they were too much of a reminder of what I was trying to block out. So, without consciously realizing it, I became a doctor and a teacher partly because helping other people was so far removed from the highly threatening hostility that I felt.*
>
> *For a while, I believed that I had achieved a successful adjustment to life. Doctors and teachers are expected to be tolerant and understanding and avoid displays of anger, so I felt both safe and productive. But since I was working intimately with others in spite of my true feelings of hostility and anxiety, rather than because I sincerely liked others and wanted to help, I brought an extra burden of pressure to my work that made me constantly nervous and left me extremely tired. Eventually my choice of profession, made out of fear and self-deception rather than from an accurate assessment of my own virtues, vices, and desires, became highly dissatisfying. And no wonder—I had copped out by giving up my own true self, and the right to choose work that I really enjoyed and was well suited for.*

## SELF-PITY

Viewing oneself with compassion and understanding is highly desirable, for this enables a person to accept his or her own mistakes calmly enough to be able to learn from them. Self-pity, however, is a form of reaction formation that makes it more difficult to resolve neurotic hang-ups. People who wallow in self-pity actually feel a great deal of self-contempt because they cannot solve their problems, and they try to protect themselves from this highly threatening emotion by adopting the opposite viewpoint and seeing themselves as deserving of sympathy and consolation. But since their real feelings about themselves are not at all sympathetic, this temporary palliative for emotional pain serves as a barrier to self-understanding and resolution of the true underlying problem. Anger toward oneself is indeed threatening, but experiencing some of it can actually give a person the needed strength to begin to attack his or her difficulties.

### GLORY

One way of trying to alleviate painful feelings of self-contempt is unconsciously to use reaction formation and feel that glorious success is just around the corner. This may be done entirely in the fantasy world of the sufferer's imagination, as in the case of James Thurber's well-known character Walter Mitty or Charles Schulz's incomparable Snoopy. Alternatively, a person may actively seek such triumphs as winning an important election, doing an especially outstanding job, or earning a major award. But since the person's goals are based on self-deception, no amount of success in the outside world will help for long; after the initial glow has subsided, he or she feels vaguely empty and unfulfilled. To hide the threatening fact that this is actually due to deep and long-standing self-contempt coming to the surface, the individual searches for still greater achievements, and the quest for glory thus becomes endless and insatiable. In fact, the emotional pain experienced by such people can be resolved only by looking within themselves, and at the faulty learning they have experienced; but self-deception has become too much of a habit, and so they remain driven to reach goals that seem glorious at a distance but that cannot provide the restored self-esteem that they so desperately need.*

---

* This is typical of some famous dictators, politicians, movie stars, and other notorious figures. Unfortunately, whole nations can become pawns victimized by the neurotic hang-ups of powerful individuals.

### Denial of Reality

One of the simplest ways of reducing anxiety and protecting self-esteem is by refusing to accept an unpleasant or threatening fact, even though it is accompanied by what would ordinarily be convincing evidence. In November 1963, for example, many people at first refused to believe radio and television reports of the assassination of President John F. Kennedy.

Although the temporary relief offered by denial of reality is very seductive, refusing to face the truth usually leads to misguided and self-destructive behavior. Common examples of denial include:

*Death.* While it is easy to say in words that death must eventually come, most people don't really accept the idea that they (and those they love) will someday be gone. Much of our society is devoted to denying the painful reality of death. We may try to conceal it by using euphemisms like "waste him" instead of "kill him," or we may try to pretend that death is actually enjoyable by using it as entertainment in movies and television programs.

People with severe neurotic hang-ups are particularly likely to use denial about death, and act as though they had all the time in the world in which to solve their problems. This conceals the fact that their neurotic life-styles are only cheating themselves because their time on earth is limited, which in turn hides the necessity to examine the things about themselves that they fear will be so unpleasant. Therefore, it is very desirable for those with neurotic hang-ups emotionally to accept the knowledge that their lives will someday end. This rude awakening will help them to gain the impetus to attack their problems, and build the kind of life they want, while there is still time to do so.

*Personal hang-ups.* It is difficult for people to see themselves as others do. Denying the reality of one's own hang-ups provides some temporary security, but ultimately makes it impossible to identify and change self-destructive behaviors. As Roy discovered when he analyzed the experience of his father leaving for the army, it actually can be quite a relief to own up to one's hang-ups—and much less painful and strenuous than maintaining the cover-up provided by defense mechanisms.

*Social problems.* Some people who have learned to deny their own hang-ups generalize this procedure and also shut out unpleasant aspects of the outside world. They may therefore simply refuse to recognize such major social problems as poverty, racism, or the dishonesty of important politicians; and they are also likely to resent any attempts by other people, or by the news media, to bring such issues to their attention.

*Personal setbacks.* Failing to recognize that the romance is over and refusing to believe that someone you like doesn't like you are common examples of denial. Denying the reality of such problems makes it possible to ignore one's own mistakes or weaknesses that contributed to the disaster. But this is a costly form of self-protection, for it ensures that the shortcoming will remain to cause more painful failures.

*Onlookerism.* Severe denial of reality may involve the feeling that one's own experiences are happening to someone else. Thus a person with serious hang-ups may become an onlooker to his or her own life in order to reduce pain by not recognizing that it is actually he or she who is hurting. This often seems like a clever solution to the person who adopts it, but it is so fundamental a denial of self that it effectively forfeits any chance for happiness.

*The "lost wallet" syndrome.* Denial can cause a person to behave like the man who lost his wallet in a dark alley but looked for it under the streetlight because it was brighter there. A person who is successful professionally, but a failure socially, may try to gratify his or her frustrated needs by achieving more at work (and vice versa). Because this attempt is so inappropriate, it can only result in the overdriven striving that is typical of neurotic hang-ups.

### Fantasy

One way to reduce feelings of self-contempt is by imagining situations in which needs frustrated in real life are satisfied. Such fantasies can provide important clues about a person's hang-ups:

> *I often daydream about being on a huge spaceship to another planet, surrounded only by people who like me and whom I like.*

This is a straightforward safety fantasy, reflecting the daydreamer's fear of the outside world and strong need for security. The all-enclosing spaceship and the departure from Earth gratify these desires.

> *I have many fantasies about being a heroic soldier. I'm usually an officer, wearing lieutenant's or captain's bars on my shoulders, who performs some essential and dangerous feat.*

This daydreamer feels helpless and powerless to achieve what he wants in his own life. The officer's insignia and the heroic acts satisfy his needs for prestige, power, and recognition from his peers.

As is the case with dreams, the main theme of some fantasies may be concealed behind irrelevant content matter:

> *I constantly daydream about sporting events in which I create and name the players, teams, and leagues, and determine the outcome of every play. I have mental baseball, football, and basketball leagues, and keep them going from year to year.*

No doubt this daydreamer is interested in sports, but the real subject of this fantasy is power. It indicates that the person has a strong need to take charge in his or her own life as in the fantasy, but feels helpless to do so.

Fantasies are often triggered by some prior event that injures the sufferer's already shaky self-esteem. A person may appear to take a rebuff or rejection stoically, but may shortly thereafter retreat into fantasies that are designed to restore some self-confidence—often with no conscious awareness of the connection between the real-life event and the fantasy.

Since no one ever satisfies all his or her needs, occasional daydreaming is normal. But constant daydreaming, while temporarily gratifying, makes further pain and anxiety inevitable because the real problems remain unidentified and unresolved.

## Displacement

Anxiety may be reduced by unconsciously displacing feelings or behaviors from a frightening object to a neutral one. The man who yells at his wife or kicks the cat because he is afraid to blow up at the real source of his anger—his boss—is a well-known example of this defense mechanism. Displacement has caused real grief for society, as when radical types have displaced their intense self-contempt to the "Establishment" and violently attacked it—or when Establishment types have displaced their self-contempt to people honestly seeking much-needed changes and gone to extreme lengths to frustrate them.

People may feel so threatened by their hostility toward those they love that they displace the anger to themselves. Roy's case is typical:

> I used to become furious with myself when I made a mistake. Some of my self-hate was justified, since I was constantly giving up my real desires in order to be safe; but a lot of my anger was actually directed at my parents. I couldn't express that hostility, however, because I was afraid that the slightest misstep would lead to rejection and the loss of their love. And since I was afraid of getting hurt if I attacked others, I unconsciously diverted my anger to the only remaining target—myself.

In extreme cases, this form of displacement can lead to serious "accidents" and even to suicide. Fortunately, most people receive enough love from their parents to create at least some feelings of self-worth and prevent total physical self-destruction.

Fear is also commonly displaced from the real source to a neutral substitute. However, apparently irrational anxiety need not be due solely to displacement. For example, people who have been smothered and manipulated by their parents may displace their fears of them to others. These anxieties are partly unjustified, since others may treat them much better; but they are also partly justified, for the self-confidence of such people is so low that they actually are likely targets for selfish manipulation. They are likely to value honesty in interpersonal relationships above all other traits, even vital ones such as warmth and affection, because they vaguely recognize their inability to protect themselves from the designs of other people.

Positive emotions can be displaced as well as negative ones. Thus a person who is afraid of people and meets someone likable may displace threatening feelings of warmth onto a safe substitute, and become highly enthusiastic about a hobby or vice (such as cigarette smoking) associated with the potential friend rather than with the person in question.

Displacement, like the other defense mechanisms, brings temporary relief from anxiety and self-contempt by concealing the true nature of the situation. Unfortunately, shifting one's real emotions to a false target guarantees that the underlying problems will remain to cause still greater difficulties.

### Projection

Projection consists of unconsciously attributing one's own beliefs, feelings, or motives to other people. This reduces anxiety because one conceals from oneself the fact that the threatening beliefs are actually one's own. Whereas displacement retains the true feelings but shifts the target, projection goes even further by denying that one even has the threatening attitudes.

Projection of self-contempt is very common. This emotion is so painful that many sufferers unconsciously prefer to think that others are looking down on them. Projection is also at work in the case of the man whose suspicions that various people are homosexual are based on unconscious fears that he himself is homosexual; in students or employees who conceal their own boredom and desires to quit by believing that others want them to fail; in the person who blames society for his or her own inability to succeed; in the social crusader who projects her own shortcomings onto other people or institutions and then goes to great lengths to eliminate them; in the politician who projects his own fears about discovering his weaknesses onto the media and accuses them of irresponsible reporting; and in people so threatened by their own anger that they believe instead that others are very angry with them. When extreme enough, some projections may result in the psychotic disorder known as *paranoia.*

As with displacement, positive emotions can also be projected. For example, a person like Roy, who is frightened by his feelings of warmth for other people, may unconsciously project this warmth and believe that he is loved and admired by a great many people. This defense usually requires in addition a considerable amount of denial, since anyone who gives the appearance of being so "special" will actually turn off most people.

Like all defense mechanisms, projection is difficult to identify (and give up) because its selection and use are unconscious. A good clue that projection is taking place is an emotion that applies indiscriminately to almost everyone: "They're all out to get me." "Vice [corruption] [incompetence] is everywhere." "All of my colleagues [teachers] [subordinates] hate me." "The media never gives me a fair shake." Thus one's conscious beliefs about people in general often indicate one's unconscious attitudes about oneself.

## Rationalization

Rationalization consists of using and believing superficially plausible explanations to justify behaviors or feelings that are believed to be wrong or illicit, thereby preserving self-esteem and reducing anxiety. A well-known literary example is that of Aesop's fox, who decided that the grapes he was unable to reach were probably sour, anyway.

Rationalizations abound in our society, as, for example, with people who defend their cheating on the grounds that everyone else does it; politicians who justify shady dealings by claiming that it will be terrible for society if their opponents are elected; false friends who rationalize their lack of concern by claiming that they were just too busy to phone; racists who argue that their targets are obviously inferior because they live in substandard conditions and therefore deserve whatever abuse they receive; dope pushers who claim that they should not be blamed for supplying people with what they want to buy; policemen who feel justified in breaking the law because they are underpaid; students who attribute low grades to an unfair method of evaluation; teachers who blame their lackluster classes on the poor quality of their students, and so on.

There is usually a morsel of truth in rationalizations, for arguments that are wholly implausible are unlikely to serve as effective defenses. It is only on closer inspection— a step the rationalizer is careful to avoid—that the inherent fallacies become evident. And while the self-deception provided by rationalization is temporarily reassuring, the behavior that it excuses is likely to be harmful to both the individual and to society.

## BLAMING OTHERS

Blaming other people for failures caused by one's own hang-ups involves both rationalization and projection; one's own feelings of incompetence or guilt are attributed to other people in a superficially plausible and believable way. Roy describes it in this manner:

> When I got into academic difficulty in college, I was particularly upset because of my shaky self-esteem and fear of making mistakes. So, unconsciously, I copped out; I tried to restore some self-confidence by blaming my troubles on the poor college advisement system, the uninteresting professors who lectured in dull monotones, and my poor high school preparation. There was some truth in all of these charges; but, actually, the main cause of my troubles was my own neurotic anxieties and the irrational perceptions I had of myself and of the world, and the misguided behaviors that resulted. It wasn't until I received the major jolt of being placed on academic probation that I decided, at least for a while, to stop being so helpless; I took the responsibility for planning my own course work and selecting subjects more in line with my abilities, and my grades improved substantially.

Unfortunately, blaming others is typical in our society. (When was the last time you heard a high-ranking politician, employer, or other important person admit an error?) It isn't until those with hang-ups learn to take responsibility for their own mistakes that they can improve their lot and recapture their sense of themselves—the feeling that they are, at last, human beings with unique and worthwhile qualities who are powerful enough to influence their own environment. This is hard enough to do under the best of circumstances; and the example of blaming others, which is set by so many of those in positions of leadership, makes it even more difficult.

## CLAIMS

The person with hang-ups often rationalizes that because he or she is suffering so much, or has sacrificed so many real wishes, it is now incumbent on other people to provide what he or she wants. The people who are expected to honor such claims, however, are totally unaware of their existence; so the sufferer gets no satisfaction and becomes even more bitter and frustrated.

Claims protect the sufferer from the threatening belief that nobody will do anything to help. He or she doubts the affection of others, partly because of unhappy childhood experiences and partly because his or her hang-ups actually do turn off those who would like to be friends. Charles had the following experience:

> I worked with some friends on a joint project that involved an extensive amount of time and effort. I did this partly because I liked the task, but primarily because I felt that the only way I could keep my friends was to expend vast amounts of energy to help them out. Later, I asked one of these friends for a favor. I sensed that it was an excessive demand, but I felt certain that he would agree because he was in my debt. But he, unaware of my imaginary claim, turned me down; and though his refusal was polite, I felt very hurt and victimized.

### Intellectualization

Yet another way to reduce anxiety through self-deception is by unconsciously removing the emotion from a threatening thought or situation and reacting to it on a purely intellectual level. Thus intellectualization is the denial of a particular reality—one's own emotions. The common attitude about death and the phenomenon of "onlookerism" may also be thought of as examples of intellectualization. This defense mechanism is also a common pitfall for patients in psychotherapy; they may think that they are working hard and making progress because they drone on and on about their problems, but they fail to resolve their hang-ups because they do not *feel* what they are saying.

Intellectualization might actually be helpful if used *consciously*, as when a brain surgeon or professional athlete blanks out his emotions and refuses to panic under pressure. Behavior that is conscious remains within a person's control, and hence can be changed if it does not produce good results. If intellectualization is used *unconsciously*, however, it is likely to dominate the person and control his life. He may start off by shutting out only painful feelings, but the sphere of operations soon must be expanded; any feeling (even a positive one) becomes a threatening reminder of the pain that is simmering below the surface simply because it also is an emotion. So positive feelings must also be shut out, and this makes it impossible for the person to experience the joys that make life worth living. Frequent intellectualization also makes a person seem cold and unfeeling, and thus turns off others to whom he or she might like to relate. Warmth, feeling, and even weakness are all part of being human; and the denial of this humanity will prevent a person from enjoying truly satisfying relationships with other people.

### Isolation

By unconsciously separating contradictory actions, beliefs, or concepts in one's mind, it is possible to conceal from oneself the illogical nature of what one is doing and thus reduce anxiety. Intellectualization is sometimes considered to be a form of isolation, where emotions are separated from the people or events they belong with. One common example is the businessman who is ruthless at work but tender and loving to his family, and who justifies such contradictory behavior by stressing the differences between the job and the home. (A vivid illustration occurs in the movie version of *The Godfather,* when numerous murders take place simultaneously with the christening of the new Don's godchild.) Or a student may avidly pursue a hobby or sport while ridiculing anyone who is turned on by schoolwork, thereby reducing his or her own guilt feelings about a lack of motivation in the classroom. Charles provides the following example:

> As a teacher, I was as distant and detached from the students as possible; I told myself that the classroom was so different from other situations that I had to behave in an entirely different manner. Actually, I was afraid to show any warmth to the students because of my fears of being basically unlikable. I wanted them to like me, but was afraid they wouldn't; I wanted to share some emotions with them, but was afraid of getting hurt; so I unconsciously used isolation as an excuse not even to try.

Isolation can be quite a strain on the individual. He or she is not free to behave spontaneously, but must always keep in mind the situation and the kind of behavior that it requires. And it can also be a considerable strain on the fabric of society, as when it enables people to perform illegal and unethical acts that they would never permit themselves to do within their own circle of intimates.

### Following Orders

The well-known attempt to excuse immoral behavior by arguing that "I'm only following orders" is designed to reduce anxiety by enabling people to conceal from themselves a potentially painful conflict: should they do what their superiors demand, or what they really think is right? The behavior of some neurotics is similar, except that the totalitarian state in which they live is the product of their own minds. They constantly feel pressured to follow orders and don't realize that the painful commands are actually of their own creation. Roy tells it this way:

> Because I learned during childhood to fear any attempts at showing initiative and to dread the possibility of making mistakes, I approached my college work with extreme anxiety. For example, I never took any courses just for the fun of it even though I had ample room in my schedule for electives; I felt that I had to limit myself to only those courses that I needed for my future profession. Or, when I realized after the first week of a course in advanced chemistry that

*I was in way over my head, I felt that I had no choice but to stick it out—even though dropping a course was specifically permitted by college regulations. So I suffered a great deal in the course, learned nothing, and wound up with a D. It was like that all the time; there were always commands that I simply had to follow.*

*I never realized that these orders came from my own mind, and that the misguided purpose that they served was to conceal some very threatening aspects of reality. I had been ignoring my real wishes and seeking safety for so long that I no longer had any idea who I really was and what I really wanted. By always having things that I "should" do, I was able to avoid facing up to the fact that I was free—but too weak and helpless to take advantage of it.*

There are many people who would rather see themselves as lacking in freedom than as too weak or inept to do what they really want. For example, they may be unable to enjoy their own leisure time because they create unpleasant orders for themselves to follow; instead of relaxing in the sun, taking a long-awaited trip, or listening to their favorite music, they "have to" spend their time doing chores that are actually trivial. Or, like Roy, they may spend inordinate amounts of time slaving away at minor aspects of schoolwork or a job. By avoiding the fact of their freedom (to relax, or to quit), they are spared the threatening reminder that they are too helpless to take advantage of it. And this selective stupidity can be extremely unfortunate, for there may well be better alternatives (such as a new pastime or job) that are within reach—provided that the person stops hiding in unnecessary busy work and starts looking for them.

## Other Defense Mechanisms
### IDENTIFICATION

A person may unconsciously attempt to reduce feelings of self-contempt by surrounding him- or herself with important people or objects. We are constantly bombarded with attempts to sell us things through identification, as when television commercials try to persuade us to buy a particular brand because it is recommended by a virile man, sexy woman, or famous athlete or personality. Other examples of identification include readers who preoccupy themselves with the exploits of invulnerable fictitious characters such as Superman, and biographers who glory in the achievements of the people about whom they write. Identification is natural and familiar to all of us, since it begins with our (healthy) childhood attempts to model ourselves after our parents.

Sometimes even people who actually are well known (such as major politicians) are unconsciously driven to seek contact with those they regard as illustrious in order to reduce their feelings of self-contempt. Unfortunately, lasting relief is unlikely because the real reasons for the feelings of worthlessness are never confronted. In fact, such people may eventually come to feel that those they have identified with have let them down and are responsible for their failure to achieve peace of mind.

### INTROJECTION

Introjection refers to the incorporation of the views and opinions or personal qualities of other people within one's own personality. As with identification, it is quite normal for children to introject parental values and behaviors. But introjection may also serve as an unconscious defense mechanism, as when people in concentration camps or prisons brainwash themselves into accepting the views of those who are in charge. In such cases, it is ultimately self-destructive (despite its temporary survival value) because it involves the surrender of one's real self.

### OVERCOMPENSATION

Attempting to compensate for weakness in one area by achieving success in another area can be a healthy way of dealing with reality. For example, a physically unattractive

person may win friends by becoming warm and compassionate; or an undersized or physically handicapped person
may improve his or her psychological stature by excelling
at some sport. However, highly exaggerated attempts to
overcompensate for strong feelings of self-contempt have
been at least partly responsible for the behavior of such
reprehensible characters as dictators and warmongers—
neurotics who have brought untold pain and suffering into
the lives of millions of people because of their own unresolved hang-ups.

### REGRESSION

The defense mechanism of regression involves a retreat
to behaviors that were typical of a safer time in one's life.
For example, an adult faced with a crisis may become highly dependent on his or her spouse or parents, behavior that
proved effective during the person's early childhood. Similarly, children threatened by the arrival of a new sibling
may regress to earlier behaviors long since put aside, such
as thumb-sucking or bed-wetting, as comforting reminders
of a safer and thus happier time.

### SUBLIMATION

Sublimation is the unconscious diversion of drives that
are felt to be socially unacceptable, such as sex and aggression, into other more permissible forms of behavior. Examples include the person who diverts frustrated sexual
energy into art, music, writing, or sports, or the mystery
writer whose personal hostility is channeled into the safer
outlet of shooting, knifing, poisoning, or otherwise doing
away with imaginary people. Freud believed that we are
born with illicit instincts, such as incest and self-destruction, and that sublimation of these instincts is necessary in
order to survive. He therefore defined mental abnormality

as the failure to sublimate effectively. Psychologists such as Karen Horney, however, believe that our innate potentialities are basically good and that abnormal behavior occurs as a result of misguided attempts to restore self-esteem that was shattered by unhappy childhood experiences. This reasoning implies that sublimation is likely to hurt the individual by concealing reality and thus preventing the identification and satisfaction of the person's real need.

UNDOING

Undoing refers to the unconscious adoption of thoughts or behaviors that symbolically negate a previous action or thought about which the person feels guilty, thus reducing anxiety. A well-known example from literature is that of Lady Macbeth's handwashing gestures, which represent a symbolic attempt to rid herself of the guilt of murder. Like all defense mechanisms, undoing ultimately hurts the user because it conceals reality. Thus undoing makes it impossible for the person to offer any effective atonement to those who may be seeking it, and the resulting negative feedback from the offended parties will increase the person's feelings of unworthiness and his or her dependence on defense mechanisms.

## The Origin of Defense Mechanisms

Some defense mechanisms are invented by the child—although not consciously—to deal with painful experiences. For example, it is easy to learn that if something in the outside world is frightening, relief can be obtained by looking away. When it is an emotion, memory, or belief that is threatening, it is not difficult to generalize the previous learning and refuse to "look at"—that is, attach an appropriate verbal label or conjure up an accurate mental image of—what is so anxiety-provoking. Thus the child invents the defense mechanism of repression. This helps to explain why defense mechanisms are so hard to give up; it is particularly difficult to abandon a creation of one's own that is thought to be extremely clever.

Some defense mechanisms are directly taught by the parents. Roy's case offers a useful example:

> My peers in school made fun of me a lot, which got me very upset. So I asked my father for advice. He replied that I should simply learn not to care what those clods think, which is what he did when he encountered the same situation in the army. I didn't realize that this was poor advice, for the opinions of one's peers are vitally important determinants of one's self-esteem and cannot safely be ignored. So I took his advice, and decided to deny the reality of an unpleasant world by shutting it out as much as possible.

Similarly, projection may be learned from parents who are so anxious and guilt-ridden that they take upon themselves the responsibility for the child's mistakes, or from parents who themselves engage in a great deal of projection. Other defense mechanisms may be learned in a comparable manner.

## Neurotic Vicious Circles

In Chapter 2, we saw how Carol drew numerous faulty conclusions about men because of her father's long terminal illness during her early childhood. She "learned" that men would surely desert her sooner or later, as her father did; that men had no love or warmth to offer and would treat her as dispassionately as did her invalid (and hence unapproachable) father; and that she herself was in some way responsible for losing the affection that she craved. Her beliefs about men and about herself were never labeled properly, so they remained unconscious and continued to victimize her throughout her life.

To alleviate her feelings of self-contempt and anxiety, she unconsciously adopted such defense mechanisms as reaction formation (going to many singles affairs, like a person who really wants a date); self-pity; projection (believing that no man could possibly like her); and rationalization (inventing apparently plausible reasons why she couldn't possibly attract a man, as by emphasizing those aspects of her physical attributes that were unattractive). Although this brought her temporary relief, it prevented her from identifying and resolving the true problem. Now when loneliness, frustration, and social pressures do cause Carol to date, she drives away any man who might be interested in her by bursts of anger, evident nervousness, and excessive demands on the man to prove his loyalty. The resulting failures increase her feelings of pain and self-contempt, and her convictions about the worthlessness of men in general. And so she remains a lonely, angry, confused, and unfulfilled woman. This neurotic vicious circle is depicted in Figure 2.

As a second example, we have seen that Roy learned during his early childhood that he had no right to take any risks or show any initiative, even if this meant sacrificing his true desires. As a result, he turned to defense mechanisms to reduce his feelings of anxiety and self-contempt. But here again, the temporary relief that he obtained cost a steep price; he ultimately wound up unhappy and frustrated because he was unable to do his own thing and get real happiness out of life. Roy's neurotic vicious circle is illustrated in Figure 3.

As these examples show, the person with neurotic hang-ups needs to face up to the vicious circles that are hurting him or her, identify the unconscious defense mechanisms that are causing all the trouble, and gather the courage to see things as they really are and attack the true underlying problem. To be sure, abandoning a defense mechanism does bring a temporary increase in anxiety, and this could lead to a hurried return to the vicious circle. But if this trap is avoided, benign circles can be developed wherein things get progressively better. (See Figure 4.) And this will be possible once the sufferer identifies the faulty childhood learning and the resulting misguided beliefs that are causing selective stupidity in important areas of his or her life.

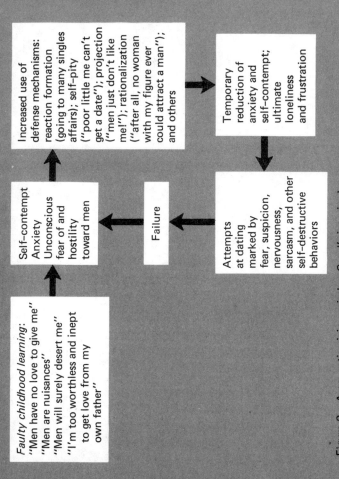

Figure 2. A neurotic vicious circle: Carol's impaired heterosexual relationships

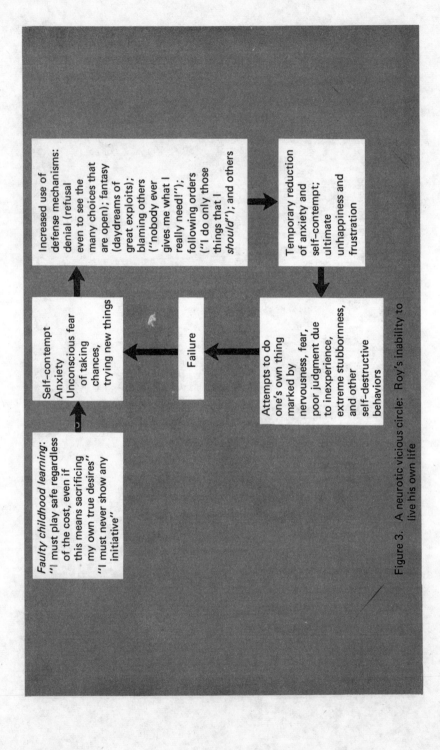

Figure 3. A neurotic vicious circle: Roy's inability to live his own life

*Faulty childhood learning:*
"I must play safe regardless of the cost, even if this means sacrificing my own true desires"
"I must never show any initiative"

Self-contempt
Anxiety
Unconscious fear of taking chances, trying new things

Increased use of defense mechanisms: denial (refusal even to see the many choices that are open); fantasy (daydreams of great exploits); blaming others ("nobody ever gives me what I really need!"); following orders ("I do only those things that I *should*"); and others

Temporary reduction of anxiety and self-contempt; ultimate unhappiness and frustration

Attempts to do one's own thing marked by nervousness, fear, poor judgment due to inexperience, extreme stubbornness, and other self-destructive behaviors

Failure

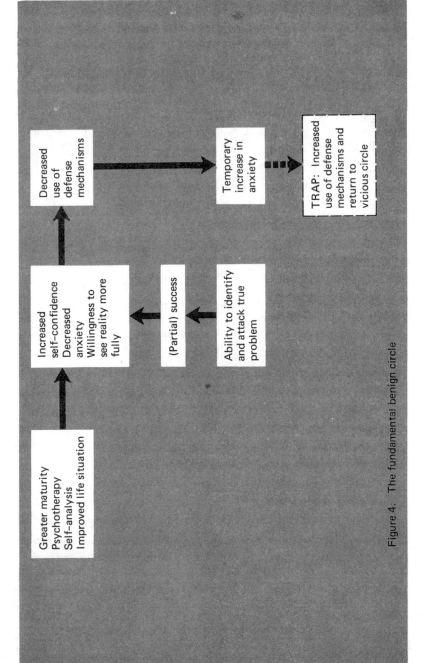

Figure 4. The fundamental benign circle

# 4

# Understanding Neurotic Behavior

The kind of safety which the neurotic achieves is like that of the warrior in medieval times who was clad from head to toe in impenetrable armor; when he was pushed from his horse he could not get up because of the weight of his own weapons and needed servants to help him to his feet again. Similarly, the excessive defenses of the neurotic make him impotent. The methods of defense can vary from the extreme of putting on a fierce mask to frighten the enemy to the other extreme of advertising oneself as a weak, harmless creature who could not hurt a fly, in order to avert the anger of the presumed enemy. Behind the angers and hates of the neurotic person fear is always lurking. . . . Most human pleasures are sacrificed as life ceases to be lived and is increasingly conducted as though it were a legal case being tried in a court that never adjourns.

—Andras Angyal,
*Neurosis and Treatment*

*Every night before going to bed, Roy feels compelled to check the alarm clock some ten or fifteen times to be sure that it is set to go off the following morning. He wants to stop this irritating ritual; but if he tries to control himself, he feels a growing worry and "just has to" examine the clock once again to be sure it's set—which, of course, it is.*

*Sam cannot stop thinking about nonsense words that he himself makes up. They seem to mean nothing at all, but he can't get them out of his head.*

*Roy is terrified of heights. He is unable even to walk across a sturdy concrete highway bridge because he will see the ground far below. If he tries, he breaks out in a cold sweat, panics, and backs up inch by inch until he is safely off the bridge.*

*John radiates anxiety and tension. He perspires almost all the time, shakes with nervousness, and looks as though he were about to jump out of his skin at any moment, all without any apparent cause.*

*Bill glorifies minor events in his life. He exults over preparing his meals, arranging his furniture, or doing some unimportant detail of his job in exactly the right way, in a manner similar to that which other people reserve for love affairs or major triumphs.*

These are real-life illustrations of hang-ups that have developed into neurotic behavior. Although they may seem "crazy" and perhaps humorous, they are actually attempts at communication (albeit unusual and confused ones) that cry out for understanding, made by people who are suffering from severe emotional pain for reasons that they don't understand.

## Compulsions and Obsessions

Repeated *actions* that a person cannot stop even though they are apparently useless, such as Roy's ritual with the alarm clock, are known as *compulsions.* Other examples of compulsions include checking five or ten times to be sure that the stove or electric lights are off or that the door is locked before leaving the house, constantly examining one's pocket to be sure that a wallet or key ring has not fallen out, or always getting into bed at night from the left-hand side and getting up in the morning from the right-hand side. In each case, the person pretty much "knows" that the behavior is unnecessary, but feels nervous and uncomfortable unless he or she performs the ritual—whereupon he or she feels nervous and uncomfortable about being unable to stop the compulsion.

*Obsessions* are similar, but involve repeated *thoughts* that a person cannot stop. Examples include Sam's preoccupation with nonsense words, thinking about a particular song or catchphrase over and over, or having constantly recurring ideas about doing something of an illegal or immoral nature.

Some possible explanations for these forms of neurotic behavior include:

1. *A compulsion or obsession may show how a person really feels about himself.* In Chapter 2, we saw that some parents are so threatened by the child's displays of strength that they react with severe forms of punishment, such as rejection. This teaches the child to be, and feel, weak and helpless; and such unfortunate learning is likely to last well into adolescence and adulthood, where it may be expressed as a compulsion. For example, by checking the alarm clock so many times, Roy is actually expressing this belief about himself:

> *I am inept. I feel so ineffectual that I can't even trust an inert object like a clock to stay set after I pull the lever. This is what my parents wanted, and what I must be to keep their love.*

It is very threatening to feel so helpless, however; peers and society expect grown people to be able to take care of themselves, and those healthy motives that Roy still has push him in the opposite direction of being strong and doing his own thing. Thus the compulsion enables Roy to express this important inner conflict in a way that hides the frightening truth from himself.*

Obsessions can also tell a great deal about a person's unconscious thoughts and emotions. For example, a particular song or book may become an obsession because the person senses that it says something important about him- or herself, but cannot quite untangle the message. Roy offers some useful examples:

---

* It should also be noted that Roy's constant anxiety contributed to his compulsion because it interfered with his vision and made it harder for him to see that the clock was actually set.

*There were many times when a certain song became an obsession with me; I kept singing it to myself, playing it on my guitar, or hearing it in my mind again and again—maybe as often as twenty or twenty-five times. Now I can see that these songs expressed something about myself and my feelings that was very important, but that I didn't understand (or didn't want to understand) well enough to say on my own. When I was too insecure to get involved with a girl, but ashamed to admit this to myself, I would keep singing or hearing songs about broken romances because they were actually reassuring to me. Or, because of my unconscious fear that a girl would treat me as badly as my mother did, I would flip about a song where a girl promises to be loyal to her man and not make any demands on him. Or, because I was unconsciously so pessimistic about ever living my life the way I wanted that I didn't dare face my own feelings, I'd get turned on by a fatalistic song that expressed a fear of dying before having had a chance to really live—and feel sorry for the person in question without realizing that it was myself.*

These examples do not imply that a person should ruin his or her enjoyment of music by trying to analyze every song. But if a certain selection (or a particular book or story) gets to be an obsession, it may very well be saying something crucial about the individual's unconscious feelings.

*2. Reaction formation may be taking place.* Another likely possibility in the alarm-clock case is that Roy actually does not want to get up the following morning because he unconsciously hates the idea of going to school, or work, or wherever he is supposed to go. For example, he may feel that it is essential to keep his job because the economy is poor and another one will be impossible to find, or because his profession is especially pleasing to his parents, and therefore he is frightened by the idea that he dislikes the job and wants to quit. To reassure himself, he behaves—and thinks!—as though he desperately wants to be sure of waking up the next day.

*3. A compulsion or obsession may be a way of feeling powerful.* Sam is obsessed by nonsense syllables because they serve an important purpose: they allow him to feel powerful in his thoughts, which he needs to do because he feels childish and helpless in real life. By creating his own language, Sam is in complete charge of his own mental world; nobody can understand what he is thinking except himself. And since the obsession is sufficiently incomprehensible to him, he can enjoy it without being reminded of how he cops out every day by letting other people push him around. It's interesting to observe how Sam learned this particular obsession during his childhood:

> My family is Jewish, so Hebrew is spoken at religious ceremonies. Once during my childhood when I was too young to read Hebrew, my parents typed out my part in phonetic symbols. I didn't understand what I was reading; to me, they were nonsense words. And I got a lot of applause and recognition from my whole family for reciting them.
>
> Of course, this incident didn't make me neurotic; it was rather pleasant, like a game. But when many bad things happened during my childhood and I unconsciously began to look for ways to become more powerful in my imagination, it isn't surprising that I hit on the idea of making up my own nonsense language—and without even realizing where I got the idea from!

Even some very bizarre (psychotic) behavior can be explained in this way. For example, a man who believes that he is Napoleon, or that the world will end unless he puts on his clothes in just the right way every morning, or who constantly talks to mythical gods or creatures in his head, is deluding himself in order to feel powerful. And this is probably due to the fact that he has learned to feel terribly helpless in real life. Such inventions do have some pleasing aspects, but they are ultimately a very poor substitute for living in the real world and sharing emotions and experiences with real people.

4. *A compulsion or obsession may be designed to conceal threatening feelings.* Compulsions and obsessions take up lots of time and thereby prevent a person from doing or thinking or feeling things that are more important—and more threatening. A person may be very lonely, angry, sad, frightened, or worried, find such strong feelings hard to

face, and unconsciously opt for the safe busyness of an obsession or compulsion.

5. *A compulsion or obsession may represent postponed feelings.* If something upsetting happens during the day, a person may block out feelings of fear even before he or she is aware of them. Sooner or later, however, the emotions will surface—possibly in dreams, possibly in a waking obsession. Ruth, a thirty-five-year-old woman, tells this story:

> *Almost every night before going to bed, I used to imagine myself tumbling out my five-story window or falling from a high-flying airplane. No matter how hard I tried, I couldn't stop these unpleasant fantasies from taking place. For a while, I thought that perhaps the obsession showed that I had suicidal tendencies. But when that idea didn't lead anywhere, I looked more deeply—and found out what was really going on. I had a strong need to look and feel powerful and unruffled on my job, because I was a woman in an important position working primarily with men. When something went wrong, or when I had to confront a (male) colleague, I was so afraid of my fear that I hid my true feelings even from myself. I didn't want to be inferior to all those strong-looking and poker-faced men! At night, however, when I was safe in my own home, my thoughts of being in danger came flooding out in the form of falling from high places. When I learned to be more honest with myself about my feelings at work as they happened, my obsession became much less frequent.*

Hiding one's feelings from others is often necessary in order to avoid being taken advantage of, or to keep friends. But hiding feelings from oneself is a self-destructive form of defense that may lead to compulsive or obsessive behavior.

## Phobias

A *phobia* occurs when strong anxiety is caused by a specific object or situation that actually presents no real danger at all. Roy's fear of heights is a good example, for he was terrified not by a rickety and unsafe bridge (which would be natural and understandable) but by a solid concrete bridge that was not in any danger of collapsing. Many kinds of phobias have been observed, such as a fear of closed spaces, animals, open spaces, and so forth. People suffering from phobias realize with their minds that there is no real cause for fear: but if they enter the phobic situation, their emotions take charge and they panic completely.

Some underlying causes of phobias are:

1. *A phobia may indicate that strong and important feelings are being concealed.* Because of his parents' double-bind behaviors, Roy came to feel that they were hypocritical and untrustworthy; and because he assumed that other people must be similar to his parents, he unconsciously concluded that people in general could not be trusted. He "knows" with his mind that other people probably don't want to push him off the bridge, but his emotions (or unlabeled beliefs) aren't entirely convinced. Therefore he finds it much safer to stay on solid ground where people can't hurt him so easily, rather than risk a walk over a high bridge where someone—either out of clumsiness or malice —might bump him over the side.

In addition, Roy has had considerable difficulty showing his emotions about anything, especially to himself, and he intellectualizes a great deal. Yet he senses that his feelings are very powerful. If they were to come to the fore while he was in a vulnerable position, such as atop a high bridge, all hell might break loose. Consequently Roy's unlabeled but intense fear that his emotions will eventually explode makes solid ground a much safer place to be.

2. *A phobia may serve as protection against threatening impulses.* Because he experienced such considerable emotional pain for so much of his childhood and adolescence, Roy developed some vague and largely unconscious thoughts about ending his torment by committing suicide. His phobia is, in part, a way of protecting himself from these hidden wishes by preventing him from ever getting out on the bridge in the first place.

*3. A phobia may indicate a displaced fear.* Roy grew up feeling so helpless and insubstantial that he half believes that a gust of wind can blow him off a high bridge. Even though his intelligence tells him that this is impossible, his emotions take over whenever he tries to cross the bridge and he truly feels that he is in serious danger. Thus his fright is actually due to his belief that he is nothing and nobody, and this emotion is greatly intensified by being on the bridge. Similarly, a person who feels worthless may develop a phobia toward public speaking; the real fear is that others will find out what kind of person he or she really is.

*4. A phobia may be learned.* If a truly frightening event happens together with a neutral object or situation, and this is repeated enough times, the fear will become attached to the neutral stimulus as well. For example, laboratory rats who are given numerous electric shocks in a white compartment will learn to fear the color white even in the absence of additional shocks. Similarly, a child punished or frightened often enough in a particular place will come to fear that location.

Clues like these have helped Roy to overcome his phobia. He still doesn't especially enjoy high places, but he can walk across the bridge that was formerly impassable.

*I had given up trying to walk across the highway bridge, and took cabs or buses wherever I had to go. Then I participated in a group therapy session that helped me a great deal. There was an exercise called a "lift," where other people hoisted me off the ground and rocked me back and forth gently. I was surprised at how scared I was of this at first, since I was only a foot above the ground and in no danger. I began to realize how little I trusted other people, and how groundless most of my suspicions were; the others didn't drop me, and I got to enjoy being supported by them. Later in the session, I was able to show strong emotion for one of the few times in my life, and they didn't laugh at me or put me down. I wound up liking several of them, and felt that some of them liked me. Having gotten some of this suspicion, strong emotion, and feelings of worthless-*

*ness off my chest, I walked home and over that bridge. And I made it!*

Roy's story shows that resolving hang-ups is likely to require emotional release as well as intelligent detective work. In fact, true insight requires feeling as well as understanding. (This is one reason why formal psychotherapy may be necessary; feelings can be hard to face, so the help of a competent professional may be necessary to bring them to the surface.) But when true insight is achieved, it is very likely that the phobia will diminish in intensity.*

### Anxiety Neurosis

Anxiety, or intense nervousness without any apparent cause, is the main symptom of all forms of neurosis. When a person constantly radiates anxiety that is *not* restricted to a specific situation or object, however, this condition is referred to as *anxiety neurosis.* The brief description of John at the beginning of this chapter, and the examples discussed earlier, suggest how unpleasant anxiety neurosis is.

Actually, anxiety neurosis frequently occurs in combination with phobias, obsessions, compulsions, and other neurotic behaviors; people with neurotic hang-ups simply do not fall neatly into one of the standard categories, much to the frustration of various psychologists and psychiatrists. Since the meaning of anxiety was discussed in detail in Chapter 2, there is no need to delve further into the "catchall" classification of anxiety neurosis.

* If a person who is otherwise psychologically healthy suffers from a phobia (as could happen if an adult without serious hang-ups is in an automobile accident and becomes afraid of cars), this can be cured fairly quickly by using techniques of behavior therapy. These procedures are based on simple principles of learning and do not require insight to be achieved by the patient.

## Hypochondria

*Hypochondria* (or *hypochondriacal neurosis*) consists of exaggerated preoccupation with one's health and exces-. sive anxiety about becoming ill. The hypocondriac constantly complains about some ailment, or worries incessantly about the possibility of getting sick—so much so, in fact, that his or her behavior becomes a source of humor or annoyance to friends and relatives.

As with other forms of neurosis, hypochondria may be learned during childhood. The hypochondriac's complaints may reflect the fact that the parents were excessively concerned with issues of health and overreacted to any ailment. As a result, the child came to regard these neurotic fears as normal. If this is the case, the solution is to recognize that the parents' standards were highly misguided, that the hypochondriac is still living by them (perhaps from ignorance, or perhaps from an unconscious fear of what will happen if they are violated), and that he or she will ultimately find considerably greater satisfaction by substituting more realistic standards of his or her own choosing.

Alternatively, hypochondria may result from displacement. It may indicate that the sufferer very much wants the affection and sympathy of others, but unconsciously believes that he or she is too unlikable for this ever to happen. Therefore, the wish for sympathy is unconsciously displaced from other people to the sufferer, who gives him- or herself the much-desired attention. Unfortunately, this neurotic solution rules out any change in behavior that will effectively resolve the true problem.

## Hysterical Neurosis

There are two kinds of *hysterical neurosis.* The *conversion type* consists of unconsciously converting psychological problems into physical symptoms. For example, a girl who is terrified about getting married but ashamed to admit this to herself may, on her wedding day, develop stomach pains or headaches or perhaps even a temporary paralysis of the legs that will prevent the wedding from taking place. In addition to the *primary gain* of reducing anxiety by avoiding the feared event, and by disguising the real (psychological) nature of the problem, the conversion type of hysterical neurosis provides the person with a *secondary gain* of sympathy and attention from other people.

The *dissociative type* of hysterical neurosis occurs when a person's state of consciousness or identity is affected, as when there is a loss of memory about a specific period in one's life (*fugue*) or total loss of memory including that of the person's identity (*amnesia*), *not* due to a physical cause such as a blow on the head. Thus anxiety is reduced by totally avoiding threatening thoughts or memories, even if this means blotting out the person's knowledge of his or her own name and past history.

Where hysterical neurosis is suspected, a medical examination is essential in order to ascertain whether or not there is a physical cause for the disorder. (In fact, this is a good idea with regard to any kind of psychopathology, if only to reassure the sufferer that psychological treatment is really necessary.) If the results are negative, the problem is probably psychological in nature—and hence amenable to the kind of analysis discussed herein.

### Ego-Syntonic Disorders

People suffering from neurotic anxiety may be unaware of the underlying causes, but they know perfectly well that something is wrong with them; the intense nervousness, sense of confusion, and other complaints are symptoms that they would very much like to be rid of. Such clearly recognized symptoms are referred to as *ego-alien,* or *ego-dyston-*

*ic.* There are some forms of psychopathology, however, where the person is virtually unaware that the causes of the problems lie with him- or herself. For example, a woman who has been married and divorced five times may display no anxiety whatsoever about her relationships with males because she does not recognize that her hang-ups are the true cause of her repeated failures. *Ego-syntonic* disorders like this are increasing in frequency, and are considerably more difficult to resolve than are those typified by ego-alien symptoms. A full discussion of this challenging area, however, is beyond the scope of the present work.

## Other Forms of Neurotic Behavior
### LONERISM

People really do need people, but the loner does not believe this. Loners spend most or all of their time by themselves, like a person with a "Do Not Disturb" sign around his or her neck, and become annoyed or even anxious if they are forced to endure the company of other people.

Some of the major causes of lonerism have already been discussed, as in the case of Roy. As a child, the loner may have learned to distrust the parents because of their hypocritical double-bind behaviors, and then generalized this distrust to other people who were assumed to be similar. To prevent even worse treatment by the parents, the loner outwardly behaved like a "good boy" at all times. Unfortunately, this apparent normalcy kept other people from recognizing the extent of his problems and providing the help that he desperately needed. While he was putting up a good front, he was actually withdrawing his real self and his true feelings from the threatening and incomprehensible world. Thus his adolescence was self-conscious and inhibited because he had not learned to deal with other people, or even to enjoy the idea of relating to others.

All this suffering caused the loner to create extreme

psychological defenses. He spends vast amounts of time in
the safer and more enjoyable world of his own fantasies,
and denies reality to such an extent that he cannot see how
other people are reacting to his behavior. He keeps himself
busy, and thus away from his real problems, with obsessions and compulsions. He is often extremely stubborn, for
even losing an argument threatens the shaky equilibrium
that he has established and throws him into a panic. He is
frequently anxious, because he cannot completely shut out
the existence of the people and the outside world that are so
threatening. He is too suspicious of other people to work or
play with them for any length of time, since he fears that
they will manipulate him to their own advantage as his
parents did, and his behavior thus drives away those who
actually would like to be his friend.

The loner's behavior cries out for help, comfort, and
understanding. Clearly, such anguish cannot be resolved in
a few minutes or with a few words of advice. *But it can be
resolved.* The loner has sacrificed his or her real self—a self
that is warm, loving, lovable, and in need of other people—
because of the frightening but mistaken view that resulted
from parental neurotic teaching and from the loner's own
childish misconceptions and decisions. But this real self
can be rediscovered, even if slowly and even if the help of a
competent professional is necessary.

THE P.O.W. SYNDROME

Prisoners of war lead dull and monotonous existences
in their generally barren and tightly supervised quarters.
Consequently they tend to glorify minor details of their
lives, such as eating a simple meal or drawing a design on
the wall, so as to have something that makes life worth
living.

People seriously afflicted with neurotic hang-ups also
lead boring and unfulfilling lives, but they must deny this

to themselves at all costs lest they be driven to face the things about themselves that they dread. So they also are likely to glorify unimportant aspects of their lives, such as preparing and eating meals, watching television, having an interesting fantasy, or doing some trivial chore with meticulous exactness. Such people do not realize that this self-created glory deprives them of the gratification and love that is available in the real world, as Bill explains:

> *I never would have believed that my clever solution to my problems was a bad choice. I felt so great when I fixed my own meals just the right way, saw my favorite TV program, or worked for hours to get just the right phrasing in a paper I was writing for school; it was almost like I had won a Nobel Prize. Now that I've resolved some of my hang-ups, I still enjoy a good meal or television show; but I've also found that all of my previous triumphs put together weren't half as good as when a girl I like looks into my eyes and tells me that she cares about me, or when a friend shows that he enjoys my company, or when I work at a job that is truly interesting and creative and makes me feel fulfilled.*

Bill was fortunately able to discover that, unlike the P.O.W., the only one who could give him the freedom that he needed and deserved was himself.

### PSEUDO-GIVING

Helping and giving to other people can be a highly desirable trait. The pseudo-giver, however, is unconsciously trying to banish feelings of worthlessness and self-contempt by constantly satisfying the wishes of other people. In fact, pseudo-givers may even invent and carry out favors without being asked. But since their true motive is to satisfy their own powerful need to feel useful, they do not check to see whether or not their actions are likely to be welcomed. As a result, they often wind up rejected or ignored by people who simply wanted to be left alone, whereupon they become bitter and indignant.

Pseudo-givers see themselves as noble folk whose magnanimous gestures have been spurned by cruel and thoughtless people, but it is their denial of reality about what the objects of their attentions really want that is actually responsible for their troubles. Because pseudo-givers are motivated by the need to reduce their feelings of self-hate rather than by a warm and sincere interest in other people, their behavior represents a surrender of their real selves. Not only is it not commendable, it is actually self-destructive. In spite of all their favors, pseudo-givers wind up with few real and lasting friends; other people cannot figure out where the giver's head is at, and they either use or ignore him or her because they cannot relate to such a person. And this, of course, increases the pseudo-giver's feelings of worthlessness and hostility.

The pseudo-giver needs to become more *self*ish—not more inconsiderate of other people, but more attuned to their real needs. Since the pseudo-givers' behavior actually is an attempt to tend to their own desires rather than those of others, they need to find a more direct and successful way of doing so. When they arrive at the right to be themselves, they will be able to do favors for others because they want to rather than because they think they must. And since their giving will be genuine, it will be more likely to yield real rewards, such as lasting friendships and increased self-esteem.

### MISGUIDED MEANS AND ENDS

Neurotic hang-ups are likely to trap a person into painful activities that don't even turn out to be justified by the ends that are achieved, as Roy well knows:

*I hated college; I was up tight, immature, lost. Yet the idea of quitting school was so scary that I couldn't even bring myself to think about it, partly because I knew that my parents desperately wanted me to graduate and partly because I couldn't conceive of anything to do with myself if I did leave. So, to hide this painful conflict from myself, I became very grade-conscious; I slaved away at my studies in order to get lots of A's and B's rather than because I liked and cared about what I was learning. I did succeed in running away from my problem, but it turned out to be a Pyrrhic victory; all I really accomplished was to win the dubious privilege of taking still more courses that I couldn't stand.*

Other examples include the businessman who spends years doing detested but well-paid work and then discovers that the large bankroll that he has amassed doesn't buy the happiness that he craves; or the woman who takes up a hobby solely because she has glorious dreams of winning trophies or prizes (and thereby restoring her tattered self-esteem) only to wind up spending much of her time doing things she doesn't really like (which actually increases her self-contempt). The real problem has to do with their own hang-ups, but they keep looking for solutions in the outside world. Consequently, the goals that they select inevitably turn out to be unfulfilling, the only recourse that they see is to try even harder, and the whole self-destructive cycle of inappropriate and hence insatiable striving begins all over again.

Real success, of course, often does require sacrifices. A student may have to take some courses that he or she dislikes in order to pursue a desired profession, or an executive may have to endure aspects of the job that are unpleasant in order to enjoy its satisfactions or to earn money for truly satisfying purposes. In the previous examples, however, the people in question have become so driven by the need to hide the real conflict from themselves that they spend huge amounts of time doing things that make them miserable. That is, their neurotic hang-ups have obscured the need for *making the doing fun.* The solution, therefore, is to start looking for activities that they enjoy—and to stop hiding (and spending countless hours) in unpleasant tasks that can't possibly get them what they really want.

## EXTREME HELPLESSNESS

A common complaint of people afflicted with neurotic hang-ups is that the sufferers do not know how to help themselves. Carol puts it this way:

> People keep telling me to do what I want, but I don't even know what I want! All I know is that whatever I try is pretty boring. Dating is nothing special. I play handball or study the piano, but I don't really like it. I go to the same vacation places even though I didn't enjoy them the last time I was there. Why can't anyone tell me how to solve my problems?

Carol fails to realize that it is impossible (in fact, it's a contradiction in terms) for someone to tell her how to be herself. Carol *is* suffering from a serious problem, but not the one she complains about. Instead, she needs to redirect her thinking to the hang-up that is really causing all her difficulties—namely, the faulty childhood learning that has created a picture of a world in which she cannot obtain satisfaction. For example, it is her powerful unconscious distrust of men, previously described, that prevents her from enjoying her dates. Her great need is not to have someone point her toward new activities but to examine and correct her erroneous beliefs about herself and the world, and then use this improved psychological vision to discover and obtain truly satisfying goals.

## EXTREME STUBBORNNESS

Serious hang-ups can make people feel as though they are constantly walking a tightrope, where the slightest misstep is likely to end in disaster. Consequently, they tend to cling doggedly to their defense mechanisms and neurotic behaviors, refusing even to try and make any significant changes in their lives.

Neurotic stubbornness often contains elements of childish revenge. The following example from Roy's life shows

how this form of behavior becomes self-destructive because it is based on childhood motives that are not consciously understood:

> *When my father went into the army, I was very unhappy to be left*
> *with a mother with whom I didn't get along well. I expressed this by*
> *developing an eating problem; I refused to accept food when she*
> *gave it to me. Later, as an adult, I behaved similarly in difficult*
> *situations. I wouldn't take things from women, even love and affec-*
> *tion; or I would refuse to gain any knowledge from a teacher I didn't*
> *like, even though I needed to learn the material. I didn't realize that*
> *I was unconsciously using my stubbornness as a method for taking*
> *revenge, just as I did with my mother during childhood. And I*
> *actually hurt only myself, because my stubbornness deprived me of*
> *important things that I needed very badly.*

### THE ALL-OUT DRIVE FOR SAFETY

One of the most striking aspects of neurotic hang-ups
is that the drive for safety replaces the need for self-actualization and enjoyment of life; the sufferer is constantly
preoccupied with reducing emotional pain and finding a
safe nook in a threatening and incomprehensible world.
Roy's vicious circle, described in Chapter 3, is a typical
illustration.

A common side effect of the need for safety is that the
person becomes dull and boring to others. Realizing this,
the person may wonder if reading more books or becoming
more cultured will make him or her more interesting and
attractive. Actually, it takes a person who is interest*ed* to be
interest*ing*. The all-out pursuit of safety rules out any risks,
such as failure or injury, that must be taken in order to
discover things that will turn someone on; so the sufferer
stays turned off, and keeps turning off other people. And the
negative feedback that this brings from other people pro-
duces still greater feelings of dejection and self-contempt.

## AMBIVALENCE

Neurotic hang-ups can cause even relatively minor decisions to become nerve-racking trials. This happens because the sufferer has an important unconscious "secret agenda": whether to follow the route dictated by his or her hang-ups, or whether to pursue the direction indicated by the sufferer's dimly recognized real self. Roy's difficulty in leaving a boring party, described in Chapter 1, is a typical example; he truly wished to leave, but envisioned all sorts of commands telling him that he should stay. Or a man may spend inordinate amounts of time about a business decision, or about a choice of plans in a game that he is playing, because his hang-ups are urging him to please other people (and play safe) by losing while his real self wants the satisfaction of winning. Thus the powerful, contradictory, and largely unconscious desires leave him at a complete standstill. In addition, the anxiety that accompanies neurotic hang-ups adds to the problem by making it difficult for a person to think clearly or, in extreme situations, even to see accurately.

As with other neurotic behaviors, extreme ambivalence can be resolved by identifying and facing the true underlying problem. This may require keen analysis, but the self-confidence and satisfaction that results from the ability to make one's own decisions will be well worth the time and effort that are invested.

## HOPELESSNESS AND CONFUSION

Hang-ups are likely to make people feel hopeless about their ability to resolve them, a painful emotion that may well be hidden beneath various defense mechanisms. This occurs primarily because their best attempts to relieve their pain, namely, defense mechanisms and neurotic behaviors, are rising up to destroy them, yet they see no alternative but to continue down the path that they have forged. Actually, those ill-chosen neurotic solutions were determined largely during childhood, when they lacked the maturity to select better plans, and they now have much more knowledge with which to attack their problems. Therefore neurotic hopelessness should be regarded as the result of one's hang-ups, rather than as an accurate assessment of reality. Similar reasoning applies to the feelings of confusion that also frequently accompany neurotic hang-ups.

### SELF-CONTEMPT

People with severe neurotic hang-ups have a great deal of contempt for themselves, a situation so painful that they try to hide it from themselves at all costs. This is partly because they know that they have sold their psychological "souls" for small return. That is, they have abandoned their true selves, desires, and needs in order to gain minimal relief from their anxiety and emotional pain, only to have ultimately made matters much worse. Another reason for the self-contempt is that their hang-ups do cause them to behave in ways that bring derision, rejection, or other kinds of negative feedback from the various people in their lives.

When trying to resolve neurotic hang-ups, it's particularly desirable to adopt an attitude of reserving judgment about oneself. Some people are in such a hurry to wipe their slate clean that they rush to change "bad" behaviors before they have any idea about their true causes or meanings, and this haste can't help but produce a great deal of wasted time and effort.

### CONTEMPT FOR OTHERS

Self-contempt may be disguised by the defense mechanism of displacement and unconsciously turned into contempt for other people. Thus a person may be snobbish, or vindictive and overly competitive, because he or she actually is very down on him- or herself and finds this fact too threatening to face. Such people often feel as though their inability to find close friends to whom they can really relate is because the people that they meet always have some weakness that turns them off. Or they may feel that it is more important to get ahead and score victories than to develop intimate relationships. In actuality, it is their own fears of revealing their emotions and risking ridicule or rejection that are responsible for their contempt for other people.

Examples of contempt for others include politicians who engage in shady dealings presumably because of their contempt for their opponent or even for their constituents, whereas this actually represents their own true feelings about themselves; students who dislike college and remain there only because of parental or societal pressures, and displace the self-contempt resulting from their own cowardice onto the institution by clamoring for easier courses or abolishment of the grading system; or people who hate themselves because they feel trapped in a profession that they can't stand, and displace their feelings onto the profession by becoming extremely critical of its methods, findings, and members. Thus a person's strong dislikes often indicate important inner problems that are causing dislike of self.

## GLORIFIED SELF-IMAGE AND GLORIFIED OTHERS

Self-contempt may also be concealed by the defense mechanism of glory, discussed previously. That is, self-hate may unconsciously be converted into the opposite extreme so that the sufferer may see him- or herself as a glorious human being. Or this glorious image may be displaced to other people, with the sufferer believing that they are truly wonderful and omniscient and hence will eventually solve his or her problems. In reality, however, the people in question may be totally confused about what is bothering the sufferer and thus are helpless to put matters right, and so the sufferer's misguided view of them actually prevents any resolution to the problems from taking place.

While neurotic behavior may seem incomprehensible, it actually conveys vital information about a person who is sorely in need of help. When this code is broken by insightful analysis, the true underlying problems can then be identified and overcome.

# 5

# Dream Interpretation

[*The Interpretation of Dreams*] contains, even according to my present-day judgment, the most valuable of all the discoveries it has been my good fortune to make. Insight such as this falls to one's lot but once in a lifetime.

—Sigmund Freud

. . . we learn virtually nothing about our minds in or out of school, not because the knowledge is lacking but because society has a prejudice against teaching what we know. . . . If a person should take a hundred of his dreams and observe in each one the part he plays, he could then write an essay on the subject "What I Really Think of Myself."

—Calvin S. Hall,
*The Meaning of Dreams*

Dreams are a person's own "State of the Union" message. They reveal one's true feelings about oneself, the people close to one, and the issues and problems in one's life. However, the message conveyed in dreams is expressed in a language that is difficult to interpret. Instead of printed words or pictures that have a coherent order and sense, dreams consist of *symbols* that can take on various (and possibly complicated) meanings. For example, a friend who appears in a dream might actually represent a different person entirely, or this symbol might stand for a particular aspect of the dreamer's own self and personality. A physical background of cold, snow, and ice could symbolize an emotion such as bleak loneliness, or it might represent the fun associated with winter sports. Since most people aren't familiar with symbolic language, they ignore the important messages about themselves that are contained in their dreams.

In an attempt to make dream interpretation easier, some authors have published long lists of dream symbols and what they are supposed to mean. While there are undoubtedly some symbols that do mean the same thing to many people, such an approach is likely to be almost useless because most symbols are a highly personal matter. That is, a person, object, or background in one person's dream is very likely to signify something different from what it would in someone else's dream because no two people experience and react to things in exactly the same way. As a result, knowledge about the dreamer and his or her life is usually necessary in order to deduce the true meaning of a dream. Despite such difficulties, dream interpretation is an extremely important and useful method for revealing a person's unconscious conflicts, feelings, beliefs, and motives.

## Basic Principles
### THE UNIVERSALITY OF DREAMING

Anyone who does not believe that he or she has any dreams is almost surely wrong. In laboratory studies, hardened skeptics (among others) were awakened at unusual times and discovered to their surprise that they, too, had been dreaming.

The real difference among people has to do with how well they remember what they dream, and there are several factors that affect dream recall. Dreams tend to last for about ten minutes to an hour, and there are usually about four such dream periods per average night's sleep. Thus some of the ability to remember dreams depends on the accident of when a person happens to wake up; a dream is more likely to be remembered if awakening occurs during the dream or right at its end, while it is much harder to recall a dream that occurred some time before awakening. There is also a slight tendency for abrupt awakenings, as when an alarm clock goes off, to produce better dream recall than gradual awakenings. Finally, people who believe in psychological analysis and dream interpretation, and who are introspective and eager to obtain more knowledge about themselves, are more likely to remember their dreams. Those who are defensive and wish to hide the truth from themselves, however, are less likely to recall their dreams. This suggests that even if a person's dream recall has been poor, wanting to remember the dreams is very likely to produce an improvement in memory.

### THE DREAMER AS THE CREATOR OF THE DREAM

A dream is not something that just happens. The dreamer, though not consciously aware of it, is the playwright, director, and head casting official of the dream; he or she makes up the story and determines the roles. For example, suppose a young woman dreams that her father dies. She has created this dream for a reason: she may be very angry at him but is afraid to face these feelings consciously, so she punishes her father in the dream. Or the dream might reflect real and frightening fears that a beloved father actually is going to die, as for example if her father were suffering from a severe illness. Or the father in the dream might symbolize someone else the dreamer has strong feelings about, such as a friend or relative or even the dreamer herself. Whatever the true meaning may be, the dream is not an accident. The dreamer "wrote" it because she had something very important to say about whomever or whatever the father in the dream represents.

## THE IMPORTANCE OF DREAMS

It takes energy to create a dream, and a person is unlikely to expend such effort about things that don't matter very much. Thus it is safe to conclude that any dream, even one that seems trivial on the surface, is about something of importance. A famous example concerns a wife who was sure that her dream was immaterial because it consisted only of serving her husband a dish of strawberries; yet, as he quickly reminded her, strawberries were the only fruit that he couldn't eat. It isn't clear whether her serving this unpalatable dish indicates major problems with the marriage or just reflects some temporary anger and unhappiness, but it is evident that this dream—like all dreams—does deal with matters of some significance.

## EMOTIONS IN DREAMS

One good way to understand the meaning of a dream is by paying close attention to the emotions that are involved. If a dream is frightening, it probably deals with some problem, event, or person(s) that are highly threatening; a confusing dream is likely to be about some waking issue that is overwhelming and hard to cope with; and so forth.

## EVENTS OF THE PREVIOUS DAY

A dream is usually triggered by an event during the preceding day that aroused various emotions and memories, ones that remained primarily unconscious at the time because they were of a difficult or threatening nature. Therefore, a review of the day's activities—with emphasis on any events that may have involved stronger feelings than it seemed at the time—may well provide a valuable clue that will assist in the interpretation of the dream.

### SYMBOLS IN DREAMS

Although original dream interpretation theory, as developed by Freud, argued that the purpose of dream symbols is to hide threatening material from the dreamer, modern theory believes that symbols are used primarily to reveal important but complex ideas that would be hard to express in any other way. As an example, consider this dream of Roy's:

> I dreamed that I was strongly attracted to a girl I knew who happened to be sleeping in the next room of my apartment, so I got up and went into that room. This was unusual for me. Usually, in my dreams, either people come to me or nothing happens. I got very near to her and felt great about it, but the dream ended before I could actually touch her. I don't know why I dreamed about this girl, since I hadn't seen her in over a year.

A Freudian psychologist would probably conclude that the girl in this dream was a symbol that enabled Roy to hide the true source of his affection for himself. For example, he might have seen a girl during the previous day who interested him, been afraid to talk to her, and hated himself for his timidity. Or he might still be craving his mother's love yet not want to recognize that he remains tied to her apron strings. According to this theory, putting a substitute girl into his dream allows him to gain some satisfaction without having to recognize the things that he is ashamed of.

Actually, the girl in Roy's dream is a symbol used for clarification rather than concealment. Thinking back to the previous day, Roy recalled that he had taken his car in for its semiannual checkup. He had postponed this chore for several weeks, fearing that the car might fall into the hands of an unscrupulous or incompetent auto mechanic. Finally, however, he became angry with himself for exaggerating such a simple problem and turned the car over to the dealer. Roy also remembered that the girl in his dream was someone he particularly admired for being courageous and responsible, and that she had a rather boyish figure. Thus, his dream expresses his wish to reach a side of himself that he wants, a more courageous side (symbolized by the girl) that can face up to problems without excessive fears. Roy isn't yet as strong as he would like to be (symbolized by not quite reaching the girl), but he is proud of his progress (symbolized by getting closer to the girl than in any previous dream), and of initiating his own behavior for a change rather than waiting for others to come to him and solve his problems (symbolized by getting up and going after what he wanted, and triggered by his taking care of the unpleasant duty during the preceding day). And these complex, delicate, and highly significant beliefs about himself, ones he was not consciously aware of on the previous day, are beautifully and concisely expressed by his dream and the symbols within it.

### ACCURACY OF DREAMS

In some cases, dreams have proved more accurate than a person's waking judgment. For example, a man meets an apparently charming person and is not consciously aware of any suspicion or dislike of his new acquaintance. That night, however, he dreams of the acquaintance in the role of a criminal. Some time later, the acquaintance is arrested for embezzlement. This could, of course, be a coincidence, but it is likely that the dreamer picked up some subconscious cues during the meeting (facial expressions, tones of voice, subtle hints, or whatever) that actually did indicate that the other person was untrustworthy, and these feelings surfaced during the night in his dream.

However, it would be a serious error to assume that the world of dreams must correspond to the world of reality. Rather, a dream tends to show how the dreamer sees the world and the people in it. A person whom the dreamer thinks of as hateful, stingy, or whatever, and hence dreams of in that way, may be someone whom the dreamer has completely misjudged and who is actually friendly or generous. For example, the girl in Roy's dream may not really be as courageous as he thinks. The dream, and his use of her as a symbol, is based on *his belief* that she is a strong person. Of course, if his opinion derives from solid information, it may very well be true, but it does not have to be correct just because he dreamed it that way. Dream judgments are important primarily because the dreamer believes them to be true, so they will strongly influence the way that he or she behaves in the waking world.

### NIGHTMARES AS FEAR OR PUNISHMENT DREAMS

Most people know from first-hand experience how unpleasant nightmares can be; these dreams may even seem so real that they appear to continue after the dreamer wakes up. A nightmare may indicate a strong but largely unconscious fear about some aspect of the dreamer's life, or it may be the dreamer's method of self-punishment for guilt that has been repressed during waking hours. In either case, identifying and confronting the issue in question will help to get rid of the nightmares.

Frequent nightmares indicate that the person is living with constant anxiety or guilt, rather than emotion caused by an isolated incident or problem. For example, the dreamer may be very afraid of people and the world in general. Such hang-ups can best be resolved by analyzing the childhood causes of the dreamer's unlabeled feelings and beliefs.

## DREAMS AND WISH-FULFILLMENT

Freud believed that all dreams involve the fulfillment of a wish, and, to be sure, many dreams do. There is a classic story about a lawyer who heard Freud lecture about his theories of dream interpretation, and then went home and dreamed that he had lost all his cases. "Some theory you've got there!" he snorted to Freud the next day. "Do you think that I want to become a failure?" Freud, however, pointed out that the lawyer had experienced feelings of jealousy about the great psychologist's prominence and really wanted to make Freudian dream theory look ridiculous, a wish that his dream fulfilled admirably!

In addition to wishes, dreams are likely to reveal and clarify problems, emotions, and beliefs that the dreamer has. Also, dreams may include an objective statement of how reality makes difficult the fulfillment of the dreamer's wishes, or an indication of how the dreamer plans to resolve his or her problems. Thus a dream about failure may actually be a clarification of a waking situation, rather than an indication that the dreamer really wants to fail.

## ASSOCIATING TO THE DREAM CONTENT

Associating freely to the content of a dream may help to unravel its meaning. When Roy dreamed about the girl he hadn't seen in over a year, he could not at first figure out what the dream meant. So he let his thoughts wander freely about her and the dream, and the process went something like this:

*Let's see, now . . . what does that girl make me think of? Well, girls in general, I guess. But that doesn't seem very helpful, since I haven't met or dated any girls in the last few days. What else? Hmmm . . . I liked her because she was real gutsy; she'd never cop out. And she had a boyish figure. Could she represent a boy or a man? Me, maybe. Was I involved with anything yesterday where I*

*didn't cop out? Yeah, I finally took the car in for the checkup. And*
*that is one of the problems I've had all my life—being very up tight*
*about things that really aren't frightening.*

LYING TO ONESELF

When trying to interpret one's own dreams, one may
fall into the trap of twisting the meaning in order to conceal
some highly threatening truths. Even Freud, one of the
greatest and most intellectually honest thinkers of all time,
has been criticized for this failing.

One good way of avoiding wrong interpretations is to
collect considerable evidence before reaching a conclusion.
Because dream symbols can be so complex, any one dream
(or any aspect of a single dream) can easily suggest a variety
of possible interpretations. It's therefore desirable to amass
more data by analyzing a series of dreams instead of an
isolated fragment. If several different dreams point toward
the same theme, it is more likely that the true meaning has
been unearthed. For example, Roy's interpretation of his
dream about the girl also took into account numerous
preceding dreams that dealt with his initiative and courage,
notably those dreams where he was afraid to go after what
he wanted and did not come near his goals. Relating his
present dream to the previous ones helped him reach a correct conclusion that might well have been impossible had
he just looked at the single dream by itself. Alternatively,
relating a dream to known facts about the dreamer and his
life can help to establish its meaning.

## Illustrative Examples

To clarify some of these principles, let's look at some
examples. Keep in mind that the following interpretations
are actually based on considerably more information than
can be presented here; a great deal about the dreamer's life,

problems, conflicts, and previous dreams was well known to the interpreter. Without those additional facts, it would be difficult or impossible to derive any firm meaning from excerpts as short as these.

### EXAMPLE 1. THE TWO THERAPISTS

Twenty-three-year-old Doris had the following dream:

*I was happy to be at a banquet where my group therapist (a woman) was feeding all the members of our therapy group. Then my individual therapist (a man) showed up, looking very skinny and wearing decrepit clothes. I felt sorry for him, so I gave him a pair of my slacks that I got from a heap in a corner of the room.*

This brief dream could conceivably be about many things, but the possibilities narrow when important supporting evidence is considered. Doris created this dream in order to express something important. At the time of the dream, she was in fact in group therapy with a female therapist and in individual therapy with a male therapist. Also, she regarded skinniness as unattractive because she felt that she needed to gain more weight in order to appeal to men. The emotions in her dream were happiness with her female therapist and pity for her male therapist. And her dream was extremely accurate in that her female therapist was an experienced practitioner, while her male therapist was a beginner and hence likely to be in need of reassurance as to his own ability.

Thus Doris's dream shows that she likes the help that she receives from her female therapist (symbolized by the food that will make her desirably fatter), but that she sees her relationship with her male therapist as having gone awry because he is in need of her support. Her difficulty in facing this problem consciously arises partly because she likes him and appreciates that he is at least trying to help her, and partly because she doesn't look forward to the effort involved in changing therapists. A few weeks after this dream, and without having been told what it meant, Doris actually did quit her male therapist and switched to a different one while continuing with the same female therapist.

EXAMPLE 2. THE TRAIN IN THE PARK

While in therapy some years ago, Roy had the following dream:

> I took the subway to my therapist's office, as I did every morning. This time, however, something went wrong. Instead of stopping at the right station, the train kept going; it emerged from under the ground and went off the tracks into daylight and a large park. There wasn't any danger, but I couldn't get out because all the doors stayed closed until I was well past my destination.

Since the dreamer creates the dream, it is Roy himself who has arranged (unconsciously, but deliberately) to be stuck in the subway train. He did this in order to express a vitally important issue—he was very dissatisfied with his psychotherapist and with the progress of the therapy, and hated the amount of time and money that it was costing him, but he lacked the inner strength to quit against the wishes of his therapist. The dream shows how trapped he feels (symbolized by being unable to get out of the train when he could, after all, have written the dream so as to escape therapy by taking a fun-filled trip to Paris), indicates that he sees himself reaching true self-knowledge (symbolized by the daylight) only by getting far away from that particular therapist, and reveals that he feels so helpless that the only solution he can imagine is for a friendly subway train to help him out by running amuck. It wasn't until some time later, and with the aid of his therapist (who, no doubt, became worn out by the lack of results), that he finally was able to quit—and, as would be expected from this dream, he was delighted to do so. Shortly thereafter, he tried another therapist with whom he was able to obtain more satisfying results.

### EXAMPLE 3. THE SECRET OF LIFE

Roy also recalls this powerful and emotional dream:

*I was a physiological psychologist studying cell mechanisms. I was on the track of something unbelievably important, for I was going to be the first person to discover the true meaning of life. But then some invisible super-being put a message in my head: "They kill you if you find out too much. The secret of life is DEATH!" So I gave up my research and decided that it was safer not to know what life really meant. This dream was so strong that I could feel the emotions—my original curiosity to learn about life, the good feeling about almost discovering the answer, the awe at being threatened by death, and my disappointment and relief at playing safe—even after I woke up.*

This dream reveals a particularly acute insight. Roy's feverish use of defense mechanisms and neurotic behaviors achieved the dubious distinction of bringing him to a state of emotional death. He hated his work and his social life; he missed out completely on such vital sources of satisfaction as love, joy, and friendship. This knowledge was so threatening that he repressed it from his consciousness when awake. The dream shows that he is on the verge of becoming consciously aware of his frightening secret, but ultimately he decides that the safer world provided by his defenses is preferable. The dream is also a recapitulation of his childhood experiences, which taught him that his parents would "kill" him (take away their love) if he "found out too much" (showed normal initiative and independence). And while he is not yet ready to face the truth, the joy that he feels in the dream about seeking out important answers and his disappointment at eventually playing safe indicate that he is at least on the road to resolving his hangups.

## EXAMPLE 4. FIRE!

Charles had the following dream:

*Everything was burning up; fire was everywhere. It was scary, like a nightmare. I was in some danger, but I wasn't completely trapped; the worst part was the confusion. How could everything be so out of my control?*

At the time, Charles had just quit the job he disliked and moved to a different city in order to pursue a more interesting, but financially riskier, line of work. Consciously, he felt that he needed to think positively and have complete faith in his decision in order to give himself a better chance of succeeding. However, he was so unused to doing his own thing that he was plagued by excessive guilt and self-doubt. Even though he had a more than adequate cash reserve, he feared that he had gone too far by burning his bridges and surrendering his steady job; and this powerful unconscious feeling emerged in his dream. The dream does not prove that he made the wrong decision; rather, it expresses the doubts that he refused to let himself feel when he was awake. In fact, these understandable fears about such a major change in his life eventually proved to be unwarranted, and he did well in his new profession. This dream was therefore an accurate representation of his feelings at the time, but not a good predictor of the future.

# 6

# Pitfalls for the Unwary

If one defines insight as intellectual theorizing or the ability to follow psychoanalytic propositions, then insight is certainly useless . . . But if insight denotes the self-awareness always implicit in conscious emotional experience, if the term describes a direct contact with one's feelings toward another human being, then insight is very important . . .

—Erwin Singer,
*Key Concepts in Psychotherapy*

[A person's] knowledge of himself must not remain an intellectual knowledge, though it may start this way, but must become an *emotional experience* . . . . because the mere intellectual realization is in the strict sense of the word no "realization" at all: it does not become real to him; it does not become his personal property; it does not take roots in him.

—Karen Horney,
*Neurosis and Human Growth*

Using psychological thinking to resolve neurotic hang-ups is a challenging task, and there are a number of seductive traps that can lure the unwary off the road to self-knowledge and leave them enmeshed in their difficulties. Therefore, let's take a close look at some of these potential pitfalls.

## Analyzing Other People

Only a competent professional should attempt to analyze another person. Everyone quite naturally resents "wise guys" who show off how much they think they know (and how little they think other people know) by analyzing everyone in sight. Also, it's impossible to analyze people who don't want to learn about themselves. And even if someone is looking for help, psychotherapy is a deceptively difficult task that requires extensive training. In fact, analyzing other people often indicates that the person is trying to avoid looking at his or her own hang-ups by displacing the sphere of investigation to someone else—and thus is yet another example of a self-destructive defense mechanism.

## Keeping Hang-ups by Excusing Them

Some people use their knowledge of psychology to justify their hang-ups rather than to change them. These people may argue that they cannot be blamed for their behavior, even that which injures other people, because they are afflicted by extremely faulty childhood learning (or strong defense mechanisms, or deep unconscious conflicts, or whatever). Although this may sound impressive, it is actually a rationalization designed to keep them from having to face their true problems.

Having hang-ups does not, of course, give anyone the right to injure other people. Furthermore, the negative feedback that results from being inconsiderate or thoughtless will only deepen the sufferer's self-contempt, increase the dependence on defense mechanisms (such as denial of how others really feel), and make resolving the hang-ups that much harder. To be sure, there are likely to be times when resolving one's hang-ups does lead to behaviors that are good for the person but frowned upon by others. (For example, a person used to being a scapegoat may begin to show some self-assertion.) But priding oneself on one's hang-ups, or expecting other people to tolerate any behavior at all, is a serious pitfall that will prevent a person from resolving his or her hang-ups and gaining a more satisfying life.

## Misunderstanding the Nature of Insights

Being able to talk intelligently about hang-ups and their causes is not enough; it is also necessary to experience these insights on an emotional level. For example, Roy was able to admit that he was an overly suspicious person, but this intellectual knowledge didn't do him much good. It wasn't until the "lift" experience (described in Chapter 4) enabled him to *feel* his distrust very deeply and clearly that he was able to understand this hang-up well enough to make real progress.

Even when a true insight is obtained (one that involves both intellectual knowledge and feeling), this by itself will not be enough to change a person's life. As with any new learning, it will take time and effort to refine this new knowledge and determine how best to apply it. Charles's insight about his dislike for his teaching job (described in Chapter 3) was both highly surprising and extremely valuable, but he was still faced with the task of determining what other alternatives existed and of trying out various possibilities in order to see what he really wanted. The insight cleared away the faulty learning that had convinced him that he must keep his present job in order to hide his own hostilities and angers from himself, and to satisfy his parents; thus it freed him of his selective stupidity so that he could apply his full ability to the problem of finding an enjoyable job. But it did not, and could not, solve the problem for him by magically creating the new job that he desired. Similarly, Roy was able to rid himself of the faulty idea that all people are dangerous and out to manipulate him; but even after gaining this insight, he still needed to practice skills in making friends and relating to other people. True insights clear the decks for appropriate and intelligent action, but they do not in and of themselves bring instantaneous solutions to a person's difficulties.

### Looking in the Outside World for Solutions to One's Inner Hang-ups

As we have seen, some people look for solutions to their inner hang-ups in the outside world. Examples include the politician who tries to alleviate unconscious self-contempt by winning an election, the executive who tries to hide self-hate by moving further and further up the ladder, the student who devotes great effort to hated schoolwork rather than face up to the possibility of leaving school, and so on. In such instances, no amount of satisfaction obtained in the outside world will last for long. The self-contempt resulting from faulty learning in childhood remains unresolved, so the sufferer must keep on trying for still greater triumphs. And the overdriven striving that results from such neurotic drives only brings eventual misery for all concerned.

### Attributing Behavior to Outside Sources

Some individuals excuse their hang-ups by arguing that their behavior is beyond their control. They may exaggerate the importance of heredity by claiming that people are born with strong instincts and therefore simply cannot help themselves, or they may subscribe to unproven and farfetched determinants of behavior such as astrology or occult possession. In actuality, these beliefs are rationalizations designed to reduce anxiety by allowing the person to attribute his behavior to an outside source. We all want and need to think well of ourselves; and, if we are backed far enough into a corner, we will invent the most improbable theories in order to do so. Unfortunately, this prevents the person from tackling and resolving the real problem—namely, the unconscious beliefs and emotions and the faulty learning that caused them—and thus condemn him or her to a life that won't get any better.

People have the innate capacity and the desire to be good, productive, and self-actualizing human beings; neurotic and self-destructive behavior results from misguided attempts to preserve self-esteem that was shattered very early in life. Thus people do have the power to change their behavior and their lives—provided that they don't surrender their innate abilities by succumbing to the belief that their behavior is totally predetermined by hereditary, religious, or mystical sources.*

### Regarding Self-Knowledge as All Pleasure or All Pain

Learning new truths about oneself is likely to have its painful moments, since breaking through a defense mechanism will often bring a temporary increase in anxiety. However, many people find that their real faults and guilts are actually less severe than they had imagined. Roy, for example, was convinced that he was cowardly and stupid partly because of a situation in his early childhood that would have been hard for even an adult to handle. (See Chapter 2.) Once he was willing to face up to his own role in the event and the subsequent difficulties that it caused, he found the truth a great relief. So long as people are neither too quick to condemn themselves for whatever they might discover nor too eager to blame everything on other people, acquir-

* Some psychologists also commit this error. They try to limit the field of psychology to objective phenomena in the (unconscious) hope that, by ruling out the study of the unconscious, they will no longer have to worry about delving into the hang-ups that they sense they have.

ing new self-knowledge will often become a truly reward-
ing experience.

### Regarding Psychological Analysis as an End Rather Than a Means

Psychological analysis is not intended as a permanent
replacement for *being* oneself; the ultimate goal is to enable
people to do their own thing warmly and spontaneously,
without having to think through every move. Thus analysis
substitutes for spontaneous feelings until such time as the
erroneous emotions and beliefs caused by faulty childhood
learning have been replaced with ones that are appropriate
and trustworthy. It is an extremely valuable tool, but it is
not an end in itself. Used properly, it will tend to eliminate
its own reason for being by enabling a person to become
more real and human.

### Shunning Formal Psychotherapy

Psychotherapy is in most cases a major undertaking,
and it is also a fallible one. However, it has helped many
people—often a great deal. A person has only one life to
live; and if it is filled with emotional pain and suffering, he
or she should investigate this important possibility.

# 7

# Understanding and Using Psychotherapy

Correctly seen, psychotherapy is the first scientific attempt to make people happy.

—Reuben Fine

. . . there is nothing worse than a sleepy therapist listening to a sleepy patient. A sense of vitality should pervade the therapeutic hour from beginning to end . . . A person is spending a great deal of time and money on treatment; in his life much depends on whether or not he gets well. . . . Imagine a busy person making all sorts of arrangements to fit in his therapeutic appointments, rushing to be on time, and then spending the hour yawning and feeling bored. Of all falsifications of reality this is one of the most fantastic.

—Andras Angyal,
*Neurosis and Treatment*

A person whose life is largely successful and satisfying undoubtedly does not need formal psychotherapy; no one ever resolves all neurotic hang-ups. If, on the other hand, a person remains afflicted with considerable pain and anxiety, he or she should seriously consider teaming up with a competent professional. Since psychotherapy is a threatening prospect for most people, they are likely to be selectively stupid with regard to such crucial matters as choosing, remaining with, or leaving a psychotherapist. These are among the most important decisions that a person ever makes; yet, because judgment is impaired by anxiety, it is not unusual for a person to decide about psychotherapy with a fraction of the care or research that is devoted to buying a toaster or television set. And psychotherapy is more likely to be effective if the prospective user is well informed and makes a knowledgeable choice of therapies and therapists.

## Basic Considerations
### INSIGHT vs. BEHAVIOR THERAPY

*Insight therapy* is based on principles similar to those discussed in this book. It is designed to help people gain an understanding as to the nature and causes of their problems, and to use this knowledge to achieve lasting changes in their personality and life. Insight therapy usually stresses the importance of the unconscious as a determinant of behavior and therefore concentrates on methods for bringing unconscious material to consciousness. Most forms of insight therapy also emphasize the significance of events in infancy, childhood, and adolescence as determinants of adult behavior; studying the past is not an end in itself, but is regarded as essential in order to understand and hence change present behavior. There are some insight therapies, however, that prefer to deal only with the person's present behavior and experience in the here and now.

*Behavior therapy* does not agree that understanding is necessary for psychotherapy to be effective. Based on principles of learning obtained from experimental psychology, behavior therapy is designed to remove a person's painful symptoms or modify his or her behavior without necessarily giving insight into the reasons for the problems. It minimizes the importance of the unconscious and of early childhood experiences and may even ignore these areas entirely. Instead, symptoms are regarded as relatively isolated aspects of personality that can be treated by concentrating on present behavior. A person in behavior therapy may be rewarded for desirable behaviors, be punished for undesirable ones, imagine him- or herself in frightening situations and then practice previously taught techniques of relaxation, be taught how to behave more assertively, or be given a desired object in the presence of a feared stimulus so that the pleasurable responses will overcome irrational anxieties.

In recent years, psychologists have engaged in heated debates about the relative merits of insight therapy and behavior therapy. Arguments have flown back and forth, accompanied by impassioned and detailed examples of people who were getting nowhere (or perhaps even worse) in one form of therapy and then achieved spectacular results in the other. Actually, as is so often the case in any major controversy, there is merit on both sides. Because behavior therapy is based on relatively simple aspects of learning and deals with tangible factors such as symptoms and specific behaviors, it can be helpful with relatively simple forms of psychological disorder (such as phobias) or with people who lack the verbal ability required by insight therapy. On the other hand, insight therapy is preferable when the disorder pervades one's entire personality and hence is too diffuse and intangible for specific solutions, as when a person is suffering from anxiety neurosis or from a shattered sense of self. Insight therapy is also the best way for a person to obtain self-knowledge and understanding as to the true nature of one's problems. Thus the choice depends partly on the kind of disorder that a person has, which requires the opinion of a competent professional, and partly on the person's own desires and objectives.

## INDIVIDUAL *vs.* GROUP THERAPY

In *individual therapy,* a person meets privately with the therapist (for either insight or behavior therapy) from one to five times per week, with each session usually lasting approximately one hour. In *group therapy,* a number of people (usually from five to ten) meet together with one therapist (or sometimes two), usually for one weekly session of about two hours. Group therapy is usually insight therapy, although techniques of behavior therapy may be used to help break down intellectualization and promote true insight.

Group therapy is well regarded by most modern psychologists, although not for all kinds of problems. It is more "real" than individual therapy because other people are present, and interactions with them are likely to provide tangible and extremely useful evidence about a person's behavior, emotions, and beliefs. Also, a knowledgeable therapist can conduct valuable exercises, such as the "lift" procedure used with Roy (Chapter 4), that require a number of people and hence are not possible in individual therapy. Furthermore, group therapy is usually less expensive than individual therapy and is thus within the reach of more people. However, confidentiality cannot be guaranteed in group therapy; unlike the therapist, the other people are not bound by a professional ethic to maintain secrecy. Some therapists therefore recommend that a person in group therapy should also participate in a weekly session of individual therapy, so as to have the opportunity to explore and develop matters that are as yet too intimate to reveal to the group.

A sharp distinction must be drawn between group therapy and *encounter groups.* Group therapy takes place in a therapist's office, is comprised of people who are suffering from neurotic hang-ups, follows established techniques of insight (and perhaps behavior) therapy, and may continue for a year or more. Encounter groups may meet at a resort that is trying to attract customers by cashing in on the popularity of psychology, may last for as little as a single weekend, and often involve techniques designed to give the group a thrill rather than promote any real self-understanding. These groups are supposedly made up of people who are not psychotic or seriously neurotic and are seeking personal growth and development; but since the screening for admission to such groups is often inadequate or nonexistent, they are likely to contain people who actually are in need of formal psychotherapy. Thus, unlike group therapy, encounter groups are highly controversial—and potentially dangerous. They may well have value when conducted under carefully controlled conditions and run by a highly competent professional; but in most other cases, they are all too likely to arouse strong emotions that are left hanging either because the encounter group ends too quickly or because the leader is too incompetent to deal with them. Many encounter groups, therefore, are little more than attempts at financial exploitation or phony imitations of group therapy that have even led to such disastrous outcomes as suicides. They are definitely not a substitute for group therapy, nor can they be recommended as a form of social entertainment.

### PSYCHOLOGISTS vs. PSYCHIATRISTS

A *psychiatrist* is a specialist in abnormal behavior who holds a medical degree and is therefore permitted to administer medication. A *clinical psychologist* is also a specialist in abnormal behavior, but holds a Ph.D. degree in psychology and is not permitted to administer medication. There is no appreciable difference between psychologists and psychiatrists insofar as ability, quality of training, or kind of treatment is concerned. And since most psychologists (and

most patients) have ready access to a physician in the event
that medication becomes a possibility, there is no reason to
be influenced by this particular distinction. In fact, there
are practitioners with degrees in such areas as social work
who are performing first-rate psychotherapy.

## Psychoanalysis

Whereas *psychotherapy* is a general term referring to
any procedure for treating psychological disorders, *psychoanalysis* refers to a specific procedure developed by Sigmund Freud at the turn of the century. Psychoanalysis has
declined in popularity in more recent years, but psychoanalytic principles remain powerful tools for understanding
human behavior and its determinants.

### PHYSICAL FACTORS

Psychoanalysis is extremely expensive and time-consuming. The patient meets with the analyst four or five
times per week, for approximately fifty minutes (and for up
to sixty dollars) per session, for a period that usually runs
into several years.

The patient in psychoanalysis reclines on a couch
while the analyst sits to the rear, out of view. This procedure, which is unique to psychoanalysis and has become a
popular symbol of it, is used partly to prevent the patient
from being unduly influenced by any facial expressions or
physical movements that the analyst cannot control. It also
enables the patient to relax physically and devote all ener-
gies to the difficult mental tasks that are required.

### FREE ASSOCIATION

While reclining on the couch, the patient is required to
say whatever comes to mind, no matter how irrelevant, em-

barrassing, or silly it may seem. This procedure, called *free association,* is designed to circumvent the patient's defense mechanisms and ultimately lead to the unconscious conflicts, emotions, motives, and beliefs. While the patient free-associates (or tries to), the analyst is likely to remain silent for long periods of time. Even questions that the patient may ask are treated as part of the association process and do not require an answer.

### RESISTANCE

Free association does not proceed smoothly. Instead, the patient makes many attempts to evade it. These may include long silences, telling carefully structured stories rather than letting thoughts flow freely and uninhibitedly, avoiding important topics, or even avoiding therapy by being late or absent. Such *resistances* represent unconscious efforts to frustrate the success of the therapy. They are an expression of the patient's attempt to accomplish impossible and contradictory objectives—to be in therapy and thereby gain its benefits, yet not to be in therapy so as to avoid its threatening aspects.

Freud believed that resistances are a way of trying to keep the illicit behaviors that, according to his theory, all of us are instinctively driven to express. Many modern psychologists, however, reject this explanation because they believe our innate instincts to be basically good and aimed at self-actualization. Instead, they regard resistance as a misguided attempt at healthy behavior, one that tries to maintain the only method of adjusting to life that the person has ever been able to find. That is, the patient's resistances are an effort to hold on to safe behaviors and modes of thought that were at least partly life-furthering at some earlier time in his or her life.

Resistance is a common occurrence in insight therapy. While it is primarily a hindrance to the therapeutic process, the interpretation of resistances can be highly informative and lead to valuable insights.

### TRANSFERENCE

*Transference* refers to emotions or behaviors that the patient unconsciously displaces from other important people in his or her life to the analyst. Since the analyst is an authority figure, the patient is likely to transfer feelings (especially ones common during childhood) from other powerful people such as the parents. For example, a person who was "spoiled" by the parents may constantly expect miracles from the analyst without having to work at the analysis. Or a person exposed to numerous double-bind messages during childhood may distrust everything the analyst says and does. Or a person who is very timid (or aggressive) because the parents were intimidating (or submissive) may be constantly meek and deferential (or hostile and aggressive) toward the analyst. In fact, psychoanalysis deliberately seeks to create a *transference neurosis* wherein the patient's relationship to the analyst becomes more important than the original problems that he or she entered analysis in order to solve.

Transference neurosis is a controversial procedure unique to psychoanalysis. Transferences, however, occur in all forms of insight therapy and are likely to lead to valuable insights. And transference makes possible the patient's attachment to the analyst, which is generally regarded as essential for positive therapeutic change to occur.

### INTERPRETATION

When sufficient information has been obtained, the analyst will offer *interpretations* designed to reveal or clarify important facts about the patient and his or her problems. The interpretations may be aimed at revealing resistances that are impeding the free-association process. The patient is shown that he or she is avoiding the issue and in what way, with the goal of enabling the patient to discover for him- or herself just what the threatening problem actually is. Or an interpretation may be more direct, dealing with information about the patient's life and providing insight as to the nature of the conflicts, motives, emotions, and problems that are involved. Interpretation is an important aspect of most forms of insight therapy.

### DREAM ANALYSIS

Freud is regarded as the first person to formalize techniques of dream analysis, which he presented in his classic *The Interpretation of Dreams.* Dream analysis plays a major role in many varieties of insight therapy, although, as indicated in Chapter 5, some of Freud's theories have been revised and improved upon by modern psychologists.

### WORKING THROUGH

As is the case with all learning, insights gained through psychoanalysis must be practiced in order to integrate them effectively into one's everyday life. This process, called *working through,* occurs when a person gradually becomes convinced of the existence of formerly unconscious conflicts, emotions, beliefs, or motives, learns to avoid repressing them, and refines the new insights and knowledge into appropriate behavior that will help correct his or her difficulties. As we have seen, insights alone are insufficient; working through is also necessary in order to bring about the changes that the person is seeking.

### COUNTERTRANSFERENCE

*Countertransference* refers to emotions or behaviors that the therapist unconsciously displaces from other important people in his or her life to the patient. It is likely to be harmful to the therapy because it prevents the therapist from perceiving the patient accurately and responding appropriately. Because countertransference, or any serious hang-up that the therapist may have, will adversely affect the therapy, analysts and therapists are expected to go through extensive treatment themselves before they begin to practice.

### CRITICISMS OF PSYCHOANALYSIS

Restructuring and remaking one's personality is a difficult undertaking, albeit one that can yield rich benefits when it is successful. Thus some people have found psychoanalysis to be extremely valuable. However, the required expenditure in time and money is beyond the reach of most people.

There have also been increasing criticisms that psychoanalysis is unnecessarily slow and wasteful. Many theorists regard free association as an overly time-consuming and roundabout method for bringing unconscious material to consciousness and developing insights. Overcommitment to Freudian theory has led some analysts into errors in interpretation, or caused them to reject newer psychotherapeutic techniques that might well have speeded up treatment. The analyst's expectation that therapy will last for years may well become a self-fulfilling prophecy, where he or she unconsciously behaves in ways that lengthen treatment unnecessarily because of theoretical convictions that psychoanalysis is usually a lengthy process. The artificiality of psychoanalysis may work to the detriment of patients with a shattered sense of self and feelings of unreality, who may well regard such procedures as free association and the analyst sitting out of sight as a game all too similar to parental double-bind behaviors. Such patients, having been denied the opportunity to learn during childhood what warm interpersonal relationships are really like, are likely to need a form of treatment that is more real and human in order to gain a truly corrective relearning experience. And the analyst's frequent silences may have a detrimental effect by serving as behavioral evidence to the patient that there is no hurry to get well, thus actually reducing the patient's motivation to work at the analysis.

For these and other reasons, the suitability of psychoanalysis for most people is questionable. Yet it cannot be denied that many psychoanalytic principles are a powerful and unique way of understanding human behavior and the unconscious processes that determine it. For this reason, many modern psychologists prefer a form of therapy that is based on psychoanalytic principles but is more real and active in seeking to help a person resolve his or her problems.

## Psychoanalytically Oriented Psychotherapy

*Psychoanalytically oriented psychotherapy* is quite popular and has much to recommend it. It retains such important psychoanalytic concepts and procedures as the unconscious, resistance, transference (but *not* transference neurosis), dream analysis, interpretation, working through, and the importance of events in infancy and childhood as determinants of adult behavior. Unlike psychoanalysis, however, the person and the therapist sit face to face. There is more real conversation, and less (if any) free association. And, in most cases, the patient attends therapy only once or twice a week.

For many people, the greater realism and reduced mystique of psychoanalytically oriented psychotherapy is a more suitable and speedier corrective relearning experience. The reduced schedule may also prove superior, not only for financial reasons but because it allows patients additional time to refine the insights obtained from therapy and work them through. For both practical and theoretical reasons, therefore, psychoanalytically oriented psychotherapy is likely to be preferable to psychoanalysis for most people who are seeking insight therapy.

### Other Forms of Insight Therapy

Some capable and sincere psychologists have tried to improve the treatment of psychopathology by developing new forms of psychotherapy. Others have taken a relatively standard form of insight therapy, made a couple of changes in the procedures and underlying theory, attached a glittering new name to the result, and then acted as though they had invented an entirely new approach. Consequently there is an often bewildering proliferation of insight therapies on the market. Of these, approaches whose reputability is not in question include Adlerian psychotherapy, based on the theories of Alfred Adler; analytical psychotherapy, developed by Carl Jung; client-centered therapy, originated by Carl Rogers; experiential therapy, as expounded by Eugene Gendlin; family therapy, where mother, father, and offspring attend therapy sessions together; Gestalt therapy, developed by Fritz Perls; humanistic and existential approaches to psychotherapy, followed by such theorists as R. D. Laing and Rollo May; Albert Ellis's rational-emotive therapy; reality therapy, propounded by William Glasser; and transactional analysis, popularized by Eric Berne and Thomas Harris.

While some of these insight therapies may have real value, no one method has yet established itself as superior; nor do psychologists agree on which method is preferable for which kind of disorder. Thus a person who wishes to look no further than psychoanalytically oriented psychotherapy need not fear missing out on any newly discovered panaceas.

## Getting the Most out of Insight Therapy:
## Some Advice to Prospective Patients
### CHOOSING A THERAPIST

Regardless of the form of psychotherapy that you se-lect, your therapist should be someone who is recommend-ed by qualified sources. You may learn of him or her through your physician, a recognized psychological or psy-chiatric institute, or a college or university. Your therapist should have an appropriate degree from an accredited grad-uate or medical school; and if your state has a licensing requirement (most do), he or she should also be licensed to provide the kind of psychological services that are being dispensed. (Or if the therapist is a trainee providing therapy at reduced rates, he or she should be working under the supervision of someone who meets these criteria.) In addi-tion, keep a sharp eye out for a therapist who is known to have actually helped suffering people get better. Most psy-chotherapists have all sorts of impressive diplomas, so proven performance is likely to be a particularly valuable guideline.

Personally, your therapist should be someone you like, respect, and want to talk to. The therapist should be human, recognize his or her own limitations, and be willing to share feelings rather than hiding behind a mask of perfec-tion or technical jargon. Your therapist should be strong enough to win your confidence, and to avoid burdening you with his or her troubles. Therapists should genuinely care about patients and the difficulties that they are facing, but must be tough enough to avoid giving excessive sympathy that will only reward patients for having hang-ups and en-courage them to stay the way they are. You should feel that the therapist really wants you to get well as quickly as pos-sible. A therapist is not in business for the fun of it and has every right to value the fee received, but your welfare should be at least as important. In particular, the therapist should be trying to help you take control of your own life as soon as possible rather than attempting to keep you in therapy for many years. No therapist, however, should promise (quick) success; in addition to the fact that psychotherapy does take time, there is as yet no way of knowing in advance whether a particular form of psychotherapy will be successful or whether a particular therapist and patient will work well together.

Above all, be prepared to take some time and evaluate more than one possibility. Many people find psychotherapy so threatening that they grimly remain with the first therapist whose office they blunder into, even though they soon sense that they have made a serious error. However, don't run from therapist to therapist looking for miracle cures. If you try half a dozen therapists and can't get along with any of them, perhaps you are only playing games and should stay out of therapy because you don't really want it.

### USING INSIGHT THERAPY

Once you have found a satisfactory therapist, keep in mind that he or she can't cure you the way your physician might. The therapist is the expert on psychology, but you are the expert on your past and present experiences. It will therefore be up to you to provide the therapist with important information and to do your share of the analytical work. If you just sit back and wait for the therapist to deliver solutions to your problems on a silver platter, or if you bombard the therapist with a vast number of facts but make no effort to get involved in the thinking and analysis, there won't be much that he or she can do for you.

Your therapist is neither a mind reader nor a lie detector. Don't be dismayed about sharing your intimate thoughts; he or she is ethically bound to preserve your confidences and has undoubtedly listened to similar matters before. If you do find that you have lied or withheld important information, let the therapist know so that he or she can help you obtain insights about those resistances and the material that they are concealing.

Your therapist will need time to learn about you, just as you will need time to learn how to use therapy effectively. He or she may fail to reply to some of your questions because the answers are still unknown, or because there are certain matters that you must discover for yourself. However, the therapist should understand your hang-ups well enough to help you understand them, rather than being hung up on pet theories that don't seem to apply to you at all. If you believe that you're not obtaining much help because the therapist is far too silent or lacks the understanding that you need, explain clearly how you feel. If the replies are vague and unconvincing, spend a few extra dollars and get an opinion from another therapist. Since your judgment is impaired by your hang-ups, any criticisms that you have of the therapist may be faulty; but this does not mean that they *must* be wrong. Your therapist is working for you and you have the right to fire him or her, so don't throw good time and money after bad by refusing to recognize that your therapy is not working. And if you do leave and subsequently regret your decision, all is unlikely to be lost. Since your therapist has numerous patients and scheduling problems, you can't expect to be allowed to bounce in and out of therapy like a yo-yo. But you surely will be allowed to return at least once if you discover that firing your therapist was a serious error. On the other hand, *don't* hasten to fire your therapist just because you feel that he or she has done something that upset you. Some of the most valuable insights are painful, and your distress could easily indicate that you are on the verge of a real and significant breakthrough—*if* you stick with your therapist instead of running for cover.

Don't be ashamed of being in therapy. Millions of people have serious hang-ups that could benefit from psychotherapy, but not everyone has the courage to face them and do something about them. Entering psychotherapy is not an easy step to take, and you deserve credit for it. Be careful, however, not to go to the opposite extreme and pride yourself simply on being in therapy. Psychotherapy is a means to an end, and not an end in itself. It will pay off only if you work at it conscientiously.

Although your hang-ups may make it difficult to spot the better tomorrow on the horizon, and although psychotherapy has its share of failures and cannot guarantee success in any particular case, be assured that psychotherapy does work. If you succeed in finding a competent therapist with whom you want to work, and you work hard at your therapy, there is an excellent chance that you will successfully resolve your hang-ups and devise ways of building the better life that you need and deserve.

# Recommended Reading

Books marked with an asterisk (*) are suggested for those with some training in psychology; all others are suitable for the general reader.

Angyal, A. *Neurosis and Treatment.* New York: Viking Press, 1973.

Axline, V. M. *Dibs in Search of Self.* New York: Ballantine Books, 1967.

*Becker, E. *The Denial of Death.* New York: The Free Press, 1973.

*Corsini, R. (ed.) *Current Psychotherapies.* Itasca, Ill.: F. E. Peacock, 1973.

*Dollard, J., & Miller, N. E. *Personality and Psychotherapy: An Analysis in Terms of Learning, Thinking, and Culture.* New York: McGraw-Hill, 1950.

Fromm, E. *The Forgotten Language.* New York: Grove Press, 1951.

Hall, C. S. *The Meaning of Dreams.* New York: McGraw-Hill, 1966.

Harris, T. A. *I'm OK—You're OK.* New York: Harper & Row, 1967.

Horney, K. *Neurosis and Human Growth: The Struggle toward Self-realization.* New York: W. W. Norton, 1950.

Horney, K. *Our Inner Conflicts: A Constructive Theory of Neurosis.* New York: W. W. Norton, 1945.

May, R. *Love and Will.* New York: W. W. Norton, 1969.

May, R. *Power and Innocence: A Search for the Sources of Violence.* New York: W. W. Norton, 1972.

*Singer, E. *Key Concepts in Psychotherapy.* 2nd ed. New York: Basic Books, 1970.

Viscott, D. S. *The Making of a Psychiatrist.* New York: Arbor House, 1972.

# Glossary

ANXIETY. An extremely unpleasant feeling of apprehension or nervousness that is the one most important symptom of neurosis. In theory, anxiety refers to situations in which there is actually no real danger, while fear refers to situations in which real danger does exist. In practice, however, these two terms are often used interchangeably.

ANXIETY NEUROSIS. A condition in which a person suffers from constant and extreme anxiety in virtually all activities. Actually, people do not fall neatly into this (or any other) clinical category, and anxiety neurosis is often combined with such symptoms as compulsions, obsessions, and phobias.

BEHAVIOR THERAPY (ACTION THERAPY). A form of psychotherapy based on principles of learning derived from experimental psychology, which attempts to remove a patient's symptoms or modify behavior without necessarily providing insight as to the reasons for his or her problems.

BENIGN CIRCLE. A situation that gets still better because it is getting better. Occurs when a person who achieves some success at resolving hang-ups becomes less afraid to face reality, which leads to still more success at resolving hang-ups, which further reduces the fear of facing reality, and so on.

BLAMING OTHERS.   Unconsciously and plausibly attributing one's own mistakes, incompetence, or guilt to other
people. A defense mechanism that temporarily serves
to reduce anxiety and self-contempt, but which hides
reality and thus ensures that further errors (and, consequently, increased self-contempt) will eventually
occur.

CLAIM.   An unfounded belief that one is owed satisfaction
or favors by other people; justified by rationalizations.
Claims enable a person to reduce anxiety by concealing
the belief that he or she is too unlikable to get help
without them, but ultimately bring increased bitterness
and self-contempt because they are not fulfilled.

COMPULSION.   A persistently recurring action that a person cannot stop.

CONFLICT.   The inability to satisfy one drive or need without frustrating another drive; most severe when both
drives are high and about equal in strength. Likely to
arouse anxiety, and hence to be concealed by one or
more defense mechanisms when particularly severe.
Varieties of conflict include approach-approach conflict, which is caused by having to choose between two
desirable goals; avoidance-avoidance conflict, caused
by having to choose between two undesirable goals;
and approach-avoidance conflict, which arises when
one goal has both desirable and undesirable qualities.

COUNTERTRANSFERENCE.   An unconscious displacement
of feelings, by a psychotherapist, from some important
person in his or her life to the patient. Likely to be
harmful to the therapy because it prevents the therapist
from perceiving the patient accurately and responding
appropriately.

DAYDREAMING.   *See* Fantasy.

DEFENSE MECHANISM.   A method, usually unconscious,
for reducing anxiety and restoring self-esteem; likely to
create more problems than it solves. A defense mecha-

nism enables a person to conceal from him- or herself some painful aspect of reality, such as a conflict that appears to be insoluble or some personal characteristic that is felt to be deplorable. But since the underlying problem is not resolved, the person behaves in ways that make the defense mechanisms increasingly necessary, with the result that they eventually dominate his or her behavior. The conscious use of defense mechanisms may well be constructive, however, since conscious behavior can readily be changed if the results are undesirable.

DENIAL OF REALITY.   The refusal to believe a fact, even though it is supported by what would ordinarily be convincing evidence, because it is frightening or unpleasant. A defense mechanism that serves to reduce anxiety, but which is likely to cause inappropriate behaviors that lead to even more serious problems.

DISPLACEMENT.   A transfer of feelings or behavior, usually unconsciously, from a frustrating or frightening target to a neutral target. A defense mechanism that reduces the anxiety that would be caused by confronting the real target, but which is likely to create further difficulties by preventing the true problem from being resolved.

DOUBLE BIND.   The position in which a person is placed by contradictory behavior, causing the receiver considerable confusion and distrust. The messages may be simultaneous but in different modes (such as saying "I love you" while physically expressing coldness by stiffening or pulling away), or in the same mode but given at different times.

DREAM ANALYSIS.   A method of determining a person's unconscious motives, conflicts, emotions, and beliefs from reports of his or her dreams. Requires considerable knowledge about the dreamer and, usually, his or her assistance and cooperation.

DRIVE (MOTIVE).   A felt need that impels a person to action. May be biological (inborn, as with hunger and
thirst) or psychological (learned, as with the need for
paper money).

EGO-ALIEN (EGO-DYSTONIC).   Clearly recognizable and
distinguishable from other (healthy) aspects of one's
personality, as with symptoms like neurotic anxiety
that the sufferer recognizes and wishes to be rid of.

EGO-SYNTONIC.   Undistinguishable from other (healthy)
aspects of one's personality, as with self-destructive
hang-ups that a person has but does not regard as undesirable or recognize as symptoms.

ENCOUNTER GROUP.   A group of approximately twelve
people who presumably are not psychotic or seriously
neurotic, and who meet with a group leader to try and
achieve personal growth and development. Duration
may be as brief as a single weekend. Controversial;
may have value when run by an expert under carefully
controlled conditions, but can be highly dangerous if
strong emotions are aroused and left hanging because
the encounter ends too soon or because the leader is
incompetent. Definitely not recommended as a social
game or as a substitute for formal psychotherapy.

FANTASY   (DAYDREAMING).   Imagining   situations   in
which needs frustrated in real life are satisfied; a defense mechanism designed to reduce pain or anxiety.
Some daydreaming is normal, but excessive preoccupation with it prevents a person from facing and resolving the true problems.

FEAR.   *See* Anxiety.

FOLLOWING ORDERS.   Unconsciously creating orders for
oneself to follow and then doing so. A defense mechanism that reduces anxiety by hiding the fact that the
person is actually free to act in a threatening or frightening way, but which ultimately makes matters worse
by making any real satisfaction impossible. A con-

scious counterpart occurs when a person follows tangible orders from a superior that are immoral and unethical, rather than face up to a threatening confrontation with the superior or with his or her own conscience.

FREE ASSOCIATION. A method used in psychotherapy, particularly in psychoanalysis, for bringing unconscious conflicts, beliefs, emotions, and motives to consciousness. The patient is instructed to talk about whatever comes to mind, no matter how irrelevant, embarrassing, or silly it may seem.

GLORY. An intense feeling of elation resulting from the unconscious belief that true self-esteem and personal worth has been (or will soon be) achieved, but which invariably turns to ashes and increased self-contempt because the apparent triumph has been dictated by the person's hang-ups and the real problems are still undetected and unresolved.

GROUP THERAPY. Psychotherapy wherein a group of patients, usually about five to ten, meet simultaneously with one (sometimes two) therapists. A form of insight therapy (although techniques of behavior therapy may also be used), usually involving weekly meetings of about two hours and continuing for a year or more. Generally well regarded by modern psychologists, although not for all types of problems.

HYPOCHONDRIA (HYPOCHONDRIACAL NEUROSIS). Excessive and unrealistic preoccupation with one's body and health, and with anxiety about contracting diseases and illnesses.

HYSTERICAL NEUROSIS, CONVERSION TYPE. Unconscious conversion of psychological problems into physical symptoms such as stomach pains, headaches, or (in extreme cases) even blindness or paralysis.

HYSTERICAL NEUROSIS, DISSOCIATIVE TYPE. Loss of consciousness or identity, as in fugue (loss of memory of a specific period in one's life) or amnesia (total loss of memory, including identity), that is *not* due to a physical cause such as a blow on the head.

IDENTIFICATION.   Associating with, or relating to, people or institutions that are illustrious or admired in order to alleviate unconscious feelings of self-contempt and worthlessness. May be a normal part of development, or a defense mechanism that is likely to create more problems than it solves because it conceals the person's true feelings.

INDIVIDUAL THERAPY.   Psychotherapy wherein each patient is treated separately by one therapist. The term may refer to either insight therapy or behavior therapy.

INSIGHT.   An understanding, on both an intellectual and an emotional level, of the causes and reasons that underlie one's conflicts, behaviors, emotions, beliefs, and motives.

INSIGHT THERAPY.   Form of psychotherapy that seeks to enable the patient to understand the causes and reasons that underlie his or her problems and behaviors.

INTELLECTUALIZATION.   Unconsciously removing the emotion from a threatening situation or thought by reacting to it on only an intellectual level, thereby reducing pain or anxiety. A defense mechanism that ultimately prevents resolution of the true problem, and (in extreme cases) may overgeneralize and prevent the person from feeling anything whatever. May be constructive, however, if used consciously to overcome a pressure-filled situation.

INTERPRETATION.   A statement by a psychotherapist during insight therapy, based on something the patient has said or done, that is designed to help the patient discover or clarify something important about him- or herself.

INTROJECTION.   Incorporating the viewpoints or personal qualities of other people into one's own personality.

May be a normal part of development, or a defense mechanism designed to reduce anxiety arising from feelings of worthlessness or from external threats.

ISOLATION. Unconsciously separating contradictory actions, beliefs, emotions, or motives in one's mind in order to hide from oneself the illogical nature of one's behavior or feelings, thereby reducing anxiety and restoring self-esteem. A defense mechanism that eventually makes matters worse by concealing the true problem.

LABELING. Applying verbal names to events, things, people, or concepts, thereby identifying them and separating them from related but different entities. Many false ideas and emotions originate in early childhood because the use of language is not well developed, correct labeling is therefore difficult or impossible, and the ideas or emotions consequently become unconscious.

LEARNING. A relatively long-term change in behavior, or in the potential to behave in a certain way, that occurs as a result of practice that is rewarded or punished. When correct (in correspondence with the real world), probably the most valuable way of adapting to one's environment; when incorrect (not corresponding to the real world because of naïve misperceptions or faulty teaching), the major cause of neurosis.

LONERISM. Constantly spending as much time alone as possible in the misguided belief that this is the best way to reduce emotional pain and suffering and increase satisfaction.

MOTIVE. *See* Drive.

NEUROSIS. A psychological disorder typified by anxiety. The sufferer remains in sufficient contact with reality to avoid hospitalization, but his or her views of the world are likely to be distorted. Other symptoms include hopelessness about improving, inappropriate interpersonal behavior, self-contempt, contempt for others, helplessness, ambivalence, and an excessive need for safety and glorious triumphs, although these may be concealed beneath one or more defense mechanisms because of their threatening nature.

NEUROTIC DRIVE.   An anxiety-ridden attempt to achieve a glorious triumph, in which the doing is not fun, the goal turns out to be unrewarding because it has been selected in accordance with the person's hang-ups and defense mechanisms, and no personal growth or real satisfaction occurs. The opposite of self-actualization.

OBSESSION.   A persistently recurring thought or idea that a person cannot stop.

OVERCOMPENSATION.   An unconscious attempt to make up for a deficiency in one area by excelling in another, and carrying this so far that other people (and ultimately the sufferer) meet with severe difficulties. A defense mechanism.

PARANOID BEHAVIOR.   Intense suspicion and distrust of others caused by unconsciously projecting one's own angers and hates onto other people. Often accompanied by an exaggerated sense of self-importance and blaming others. Although paranoia is a form of psychosis, people with neurotic hang-ups may behave in highly paranoid ways while remaining in contact with reality.

PERSONALITY.   Ways of behaving that characterize a person's dealings with other people and the world in general.

PHOBIA.   Strong anxiety caused by a specific object or situation that is actually not dangerous.

P.O.W. SYNDROME.   Glorifying minor events in one's life into major issues in order to convince oneself that life is worth living, and thus hide the fact that (like a prisoner of war) one feels helplessly trapped in an intolerable life-style.

PRIMARY GAIN. The main apparent advantage that a person gets from abnormal behavior or defense mechanisms, usually the reduction of anxiety. Eventually, however, hiding from reality comes to dominate the person's life and causes increased misery.

PROJECTION. Unconsciously attributing one's own beliefs, feelings, or motives to other people, thereby reducing anxiety by concealing from oneself the fact that the threatening thoughts are actually one's own. A defense mechanism that ultimately makes matters worse, and may lead to paranoid behavior.

PSEUDO-GIVING. Giving that is motivated not by a desire to please the receiver but by an unconscious drive to reduce self-contempt. Such giving is therefore likely to be inappropriate, be ignored or rejected, and lead to increased self-contempt.

PSYCHIATRIST. A specialist in abnormal behavior who holds a medical degree and is therefore permitted to administer medication.

PSYCHOANALYSIS. The form of insight therapy developed by Sigmund Freud that involves the use of a couch, attendance four or five times a week, free association, dream analysis, analysis of resistances, analysis of transferences, tranference neurosis, and stresses continuity of experience back to early childhood.

PSYCHOANALYTICALLY ORIENTED PSYCHOTHERAPY. A form of insight therapy that employs many Freudian principles, such as dream analysis, analysis of resistances, analysis of transferences, and continuity of experience back to early childhood. But a couch is not used, attendance is usually once or twice a week, and there is more realistic conversation between patient and therapist and less free association. The goal is to maintain valuable psychoanalytic procedures while reducing excessive waste and mystique.

PSYCHOLOGIST. A specialist in behavior who holds a Ph.D. degree in psychology and who is not permitted to administer medication. Clinical psychologists deal with abnormal behavior and its treatment; other areas of specialization include experimental psychology (learning, perception, physiological psychology, etc.), industrial psychology (the behavior of people at work), quantitative psychology (statistics and measurement), social psychology (the behavior of people in groups), and community psychology.

PSYCHOSIS. A severe form of psychological disorder characterized by partial or total loss of contact with reality; usually requires hospitalization. Does not require a previous neurosis to occur first. May involve delusions, hallucinations, bizarre emotional responses, or drastic losses in mental ability. May have physical causes (organic psychosis) or psychological causes (functional psychosis).

PSYCHOTHERAPY. General term referring to any procedure that is used to treat people suffering from psychological disorders.

RATIONALIZATION. Using and believing superficially plausible explanations in order to justify behavior that one regards as unacceptable, thereby attempting to preserve self-esteem and reduce anxiety. A defense mechanism that serves to hide the true problem, thereby ensuring the continuation of inappropriate behaviors that will ultimately increase self-contempt.

REACTION FORMATION. Unconsciously taking on beliefs, emotions, or behaviors that are the opposite of one's true feelings, because the real feelings are considered to be wrong or immoral. A defense mechanism that reduces anxiety but eventually makes matters worse by concealing the real problem.

REGRESSION. Using behaviors typical of an earlier, safer

time in one's life in order to reduce anxiety. A defense mechanism.

REPRESSION. Unconsciously eliminating unpleasant or threatening beliefs, thoughts, or memories from one's awareness in order to reduce anxiety and restore self-esteem; the fundamental defense mechanism. Repressed material cannot be called to consciousness on demand, so special techniques (such as dream analysis, analysis of transferences or resistances, or analysis of one's childhood) are necessary in order to uncover it.

RESISTANCE. An unconsciously motivated attempt by a patient to frustrate the success of psychotherapy, caused by fears about giving up the only method for coping with life that the sufferer has ever been able to find or by fears about learning painful things. Includes such behaviors as long silences, avoidance of important topics, and frequent lateness or absence.

SECONDARY GAIN. Apparent advantage that a person gains from having symptoms, such as receiving sympathy from others or avoiding unpleasant obligations. Can be strong enough to hinder severely a person's motivation to resolve hang-ups.

SELECTIVE STUPIDITY. Inability of a normally intelligent person to make relatively simple decisions in areas affected by hang-ups, because of anxiety that prevents the sufferer from functioning at full efficiency.

SELF. False self—a person's belief about his or her abilities and personality as distorted by hang-ups and defense mechanisms. True (or real) self—the belief one would have about one's abilities, personality, and potentialities if able to perceive them without the interference of any hang-ups or defense mechanisms.

SELF-ACTUALIZATION. Making the most of one's natural, inborn potential for personal growth and satisfaction. The opposite of neurotic drive.

SELF-CONTEMPT.   The hate for self that accompanies neurotic hang-ups. Occurs partly because the sufferer has
sold out true wishes, feelings, and beliefs in order to
play safe, and partly because neurotic hang-ups cause a
person to behave in ways that bring negative feedback
from other people. Likely to be concealed by one or
more defense mechanisms.

SELF-PITY.   The unconscious conversion of self-contempt
into opposite feelings of sympathy by means of reaction formation, so as to reduce anxiety. A defense
mechanism.

SUBLIMATION.   Unconsciously diverting socially unacceptable drives, such as sex or aggression, into more
socially acceptable outlets such as sports or the arts. A
defense mechanism that Freud believed to be essential
since he felt that people are born with illicit instincts
such as incest and self-destruction, but that many modern psychologists believe to be unnecessary because
our basic instincts are good and aimed at self-
actualization.

SYMBOL.   A person, object, or event in a dream that represents some other person, object, event, concept, or aspect of one's own self or personality. Primarily a
method of expressing complex sets of feelings, beliefs,
or ideas in a concise and convenient way; may also be
used to conceal threatening or unpleasant facts from
the dreamer, and thereby reduce anxiety.

TRANSFERENCE.   Unconscious displacement of feelings
by a patient in psychotherapy, from some important
person in his or her life to the therapist. Likely to be
helpful to the therapy by providing important information about the patient, and by enabling the patient to
become sufficiently attached to the therapist for positive therapeutic change to occur.

TRANSFERENCE NEUROSIS.   A   great   intensification   of

transference that is an important aspect of psychoanalysis.

UNCONSCIOUS.   As an adjective, refers to processes such as motives, emotions, beliefs, or conflicts of which a person is not aware and cannot bring to consciousness, either because they were repressed or because they were learned in early childhood and never labeled properly. As a noun, a concept intended to describe the realm in which repressed material resides, whatever the nature of that realm may be.

UNDOING.   Unconsciously adopting behavior that symbolically negates a previous action about which a person feels guilty, thereby reducing anxiety. A defense mechanism.

VICIOUS CIRCLE.   A situation that gets still worse because it is getting worse. Occurs when a person unconsciously adopts defense mechanisms in order to hide threatening aspects of reality, which causes more inappropriate behavior and failure, which causes the person to rely still more on defense mechanisms, which causes still more inappropriate behavior and failure, and so on.

WORKING THROUGH.   Process whereby a person gradually becomes convinced of the existence of certain conflicts, hang-ups, or other unconscious material, learns to avoid repressing it, and refines the new knowledge and insights into appropriate behavior that will help to correct his or her difficulties.

# Index

# About the Author

Robert B. Ewen received his Ph.D. in psychology from the University of Illinois. He has been Associate Professor of Psychology and Assistant Chairman of the Department of Psychology at New York University, Adjunct Associate Professor of Psychology at Florida International University, and has worked as a psychotherapist at the Lincoln Institute of Psychotherapy in New York City. His previous books on such subjects as psychological statistics and contract bridge were well received by readers and critics alike because of the clear, entertaining, and accurate presentation of difficult material. They include *Introductory Statistics for the Behavioral Sciences; Opening Leads; Doubles; Preemptive Bidding; Contract Bridge: A Concise Guide,* and *The Teenager's Guide to Bridge.* Dr. Ewen currently resides in Miami, Florida.